CW01494384

GUIDE
TO
ASTROLOGY

GUIDE
TO
ASTROLOGY

CAXTON REFERENCE

© 2001 Caxton Editions

This edition published 2001 by Caxton Publishing Group Ltd,
20 Bloomsbury Street, London, WC1B 3QA.

Design and compilation by The Partnership Publishing Solutions Ltd,
Glasgow, G77 5UN

All rights reserved.
No part of this publication may be reproduced, stored in a retrieval
system, or transmitted, in any form or by any means, electronic,
mechanical, photocopying, recording or otherwise, without the prior
permission of the copyright holder.

Printed and bound in India

CONTENTS

How to Use the Book

The first part of the book is a brief introduction to astrology, describing its origins, basic information and background. There is a quick reference and glossary, explaining many of the terms and expressions used in the book.

The second and main part describes each of the zodiac signs in detail, starting with Aries, then Taurus, Gemini, Cancer, Leo, Virgo, Libra, Scorpio, Sagittarius, Capricorn, Aquarius and Pisces. Each sign is divided into several sections: Introduction and Background, Ruling Planet, Characteristics: Good/Not So Good, Appearance and Health, Likes and Dislikes, Love Life and Friendship, Home Life, Work Life, and Famous People.

The third part, the appendices, contains more information about the planets and Houses, which can be of use when interpreting a birth chart.

PART ONE
Introduction, Background &
Basic information

Introduction, Background & Basic Information

Introduction

This book is an introduction to astrology. Astrology is
the study of the relationship between the position of
and between constellations of stars, known as zodiac
signs, the Sun, the Moon and planets as seen from a
position on Earth, and the personality and
characteristics – and even destiny – of a person born at
that position. That is to say that characteristics can be
determined, along with personal challenges, by the
position of celestial bodies in the heavens as viewed
from where and when a person was born. This
coincidence forms the basis for astrology.

Background

From ancient Egypt to the isles of Orkney, men have
studied the heavens for thousands of years, and then
built and aligned their monuments – such as the
pyramids, temples, tombs and stone circles – with the
phases or location of the Sun, Moon, stars and planets.
Indeed, many ancient monuments may have been used
as observatories for watching the heavens and for
determining the position of heavenly bodies at a

particular time of year. It is also sometimes easy to forget just what can be seen in the night sky when the observer is not in a brightly lit town or city.

Early observers were aware of the movement of the planets and were much more attuned to the phases of the Moon and position of the Sun at the Equinoxes and Solstices. This was not just to while away the long nights. Ancient peoples had no other way of accurately determining the time of year and when to plant and harvest crops and bring beasts down from pastures. Such events were vital to their survival, and ancient peoples were far more dependent on the cycle of the seasons, the Moon, planets and the Earth.

It is perhaps not surprising that these early observers were impressed by the movements they saw in the night sky. Over time they began to see that the position of stars and planets, or the appearance of comets or other cosmic events such as eclipses, as being very significant in predicting the future, after all they could predict the seasons. The clusters of stars were seen as constellations which represented different characters or creatures from mythology, placed into the heavens by the gods. These stars 'move together' as seen from Earth, even though in reality they are millions of miles apart, while the planets move in relation both to the Earth and to the constellations. Aries, a small constellation, was so named after the Greek god of war, while Gemini was seen as representing the legendary twins Castor and Pollux.

Even from earliest times these observations were

applied to people: that there was a coincidence between the position of bodies in the heaven and the destiny of the person born at that time. Indeed this alignment would be unique as no two people, even twins as they will still be born at different times, are likely to have exactly the same alignment. This may become less so with time, especially with the advent of larger and larger maternity hospitals.

These observations, and the myths and beliefs associated with the constellations and planets, were developed over the centuries into the complex subject now known as astrology. The constellations were seen as having different associations, and became what we know as zodiac signs and Houses, while the planets also represented certain aspects of people's lives. Indeed, astrology was the origin of astronomy, the scientific study of the cosmos – as alchemy was of physics and chemistry. Although astrology and astronomy have since radically parted ways, they are still sometimes confused.

What is Astrology?

The basis for astrology is the signs of the zodiac. The zodiac, or to be more exact the tropical zodiac, is an imaginary belt around the heavens, called the zodiac wheel, extending eight degrees either side of the ecliptic. This is now divided into twelve equal areas, some 30 degrees of the wheel, which are called the signs of the zodiac, corresponding approximately to the position of the constellations after which they are named. In reality, however, these constellations do not take up equal areas: Aries is actually quite a small cluster of stars, and smaller than a twelfth of the zodiac (it takes 25 days for the Sun to pass through it), while Pisces is much larger and takes up much more than one twelfth (taking 38 days). The constellation of Scorpio (actually Scorpious) only takes seven days to pass through.

The zodiac wheel is aligned to the seasons, so that Aries starts at the beginning of the spring. Each season is split into three signs. The spring is divided into Aries, Taurus and Gemini, while the first sign of summer is Cancer, followed by Leo and Virgo. The three signs of autumn are Libra, Scorpio and Sagittarius, and the three signs of winter are Capricorn, Aquarius and Pisces.

As seen from Earth, the Sun appears to move from one zodiac sign to another, from one 30 degree segment to the next, taking one year to pass right the way around the wheel. Consequently, when someone is born at the beginning of April, the Sun is in the segment known as Aries, while by the beginning of May it appears to have moved in Taurus. In fact, those born between 12 March and 19 April are said to have the Sun Sign Aries, while those born between 20 April and 20 May are said to have the Sun Sign Taurus. However, the actual day when the Sun moves from one to another may actually vary slightly from year to year.

This position of the Sun is sometimes called the person's Star Sign, but it should actually be called their

Sun Sign. Although this Sun Sign is very important in determining an individual's characteristics, and some claim even their future, it is actually necessary to know the position of all the planets in the different Houses to produce an accurate horoscope. To do this, a birth chart must be calculated. That is not to say that a Leo will want to be king of the jungle, or a Sagittarian will enjoy travelling, only that they may have far more complicated influences and will behave in a much more complex way.

A birth chart is basically determined by plotting the position of all the eight planets – Mercury, Venus, Mars, Saturn, Jupiter, Neptune, Pluto and Uranus – as well as the Sun and the Moon on a wheel or circle. The circle is divided into Houses, twelve 30 degree divisions, which correspond to the twelve zodiacal signs. A birth chart is quite complicated to compile, and the planets need to be plotted by a professional (or by computer) onto the birth chart. To compile an accurate chart, the date and time of birth are needed, as well as the latitude and longitude of the location on Earth where the person was born.

There is more information about these Houses and the Planets in the appendices.

There are other forms of determining horoscopes using slightly different systems, although still based on the movement of celestial bodies. One is by dividing the year into the phases of the Moon, into thirteen signs, which obviously involves the addition of a new zodiacal sign. There is also the constellation zodiac which is based on lining up the zodiac signs with the actual constellations of stars from which they are named. As mentioned above this means that the divisions are quite unequal.

Sun Signs

Most people know their Sun Sign (also mistakenly called Star Sign). The following table gives the zodiac signs for the Sun Sign and the dates which fall into that sign.

Sun Sign	Dates
Aries	21 March-19 April
Taurus	20 April-20 May
Gemini	21 May-20 June
Cancer	21 June-22 July
Leo	23 July-22 August
Virgo	23 August-22 September
Libra	23 September-22 October
Scorpio	23 October-21 November
Sagittarius	22 November-21 December
Capricorn	22 December-19 January
Aquarius	20 January-18 February
Pisces	19 February-20 March

Many people will have characteristics typical of their Sun Sign. It is possible, that some will not. This can be for several reasons:
• the true nature of the person is hidden, perhaps even from themselves or masked by the Ascendant or Rising Sign, which determines the appearance,

both physical and emotional, that the person will give to others

- other zodiac signs and planets have more influence in the birth chart than the Sun Sign
- learning and experience have modified certain behaviours typical of that Sun Sign
- the person is on the cusp. Determination of the exact day and time the Sun moves from one zodiac sign to the next may actually vary slightly from year to year. The person may actually have characteristics typical of the next or previous sign.

If more detailed information about an individual's horoscope is required, it is recommended that a birth chart is compiled.

Ascendant or Rising Sign

The Ascendant or Rising Sign is the zodiacal sign that was on the eastern horizon at the time of the person's birth. This sign is probably as important as the Sun Sign, in that it determines the person's appearance and the way that the person seems to others. The Sun Sign is more the person's true nature, but this may be masked by the Ascendant Sign.

Zodiac Signs

The zodiac signs are discussed in far more detail in the main body of this book. Each is ruled by one or more planets as follows:

Sign	Ruling Planet
Aries	Mars
Taurus	Venus
Gemini	Mercury
Cancer	Moon
Leo	Sun
Virgo	Mercury (Vulcan)
Libra	Venus
Scorpio	Mars & Pluto
Sagittarius	Jupiter
Capricorn	Saturn
Aquarius	Saturn & Uranus
Pisces	Jupiter & Neptune

There is more information about the planets in the appendices.

Elements and Qualities

Each of the signs is divided into one of the four Elements, and one of the three Qualities.

The four Elements are Fire, Earth, Air and Water. Signs which share an Element have certain characteristics. Fire signs (Aries, Leo and Sagittarius) are concerned with action, transformation, the self and drive; Earth signs (Taurus, Virgo and Capricorn) are to do with possessions, the here and now, and practical considerations; Air signs (Gemini, Libra and Aquarius) are concerned with relationships, intellect and thought; while Water signs (Cancer, Scorpio and Pisces) are to do with intuition, perception and depth of feeling.

The three Qualities are Cardinal, Fixed and Mutable. The Cardinal signs (Aries, Cancer, Libra and Capricorn) are concerned with executive action, energy and initiative; the Fixed signs (Taurus, Leo, Scorpio and Aquarius) are to do with consistency, determination and solidity; the Mutable signs (Gemini, Virgo, Sagittarius and Pisces) are concerned with change, adaption and balance.

This can be summarised as follows:

Sign	Element	Quality
Aries	Fire	Cardinal
Taurus	Earth	Fixed
Gemini	Air	Mutable
Cancer	Water	Cardinal
Leo	Fire	Fixed
Virgo	Earth	Mutable
Libra	Air	Cardinal
Scorpio	Water	Fixed
Sagittarius	Fire	Mutable
Capricorn	Earth	Cardinal
Aquarius	Air	Fixed
Pisces	Water	Mutable

Can the Future be Predicted?

Many believe that birth charts and horoscopes can predict the future. While this is impossible to prove absolutely one way or another, it should be remembered that any individual has free will and nothing is ever set. Any system of prediction – be it horoscopes, tarot cards, rune stones or the entrails of chickens – as a means of deciding a course of action or inaction is absurd and dangerous. The story of Oedipus should be remembered. By turning aside and changing a course of action to prevent something bad happening actually changes the future in such a way as to create the bad outcome.

There are several theories as to why astrology may work: the reader will have to decide for themselves. One is that the position of the heavenly bodies actually does physically alter the physical, mental and emotional characteristics of an individual. This could be explained by suggesting that the different alignments cause changes in gravity and magnetic fields, which in turn influence the child as they are born. There is certainly no evidence for this explanation.

There are currently many complicated theories about the world and cosmos: that the observer can change or create outcomes simply by being there to observe. A tiny change in one place can cause a significant change elsewhere. This is an application of the principle that the flapping of a butterfly wing at one location can cause a tornado thousands of miles away. All systems are linked, albeit in ways that cannot be predicted. Also, by being the observer we create the world we observe, so there is no reason why the observer could not influence the zodiac while at the same time being influenced by it.

Another way of looking at the universe is that the

basis of astrology is the syncronicity or coincidence between events on Earth and alignments of planets and other bodies and constellations – simply a strange but useful phenomenon. Some have argued that the time of year when someone is born or conceived may well effect their behaviour and temperament. This would not, of course, explain why two people, born only a few days apart, could have radically different birth charts – or Sun Signs anyway.

Another explanation might be that people fit people's behaviour such as determined from their horoscopes into the facts, rather than the other way round. Someone who is Gemini may always be in two minds about everything, yet in other far more important aspects of their lives may be totally non-Gemini. People tend to see aspects which are correct as far more important and significant, while overlooking all the suggested characteristics which were totally wrong. Nevertheless, many people do seem be quite typical of their Sun Sign or birth chart.

Whatever the explanation behind why it may work, astrology is useful in looking at and analysing challenges in life, relationships, love, friendship, home, work, children and money. Someone who is a typical Leo may have a tendency to spend all their money, lavishing gifts on their friends and buying the best of things for themselves. But it does not mean that they have to be like that. Astrology is not a justification. Environment, upbringing and experience will always modify behaviour, even taken without other influences from planets and the Moon. A Leo may or may not be free and easy with their money, but their horoscope or the position of Jupiter in the Second House can not be held responsible. It should also be said that anyone who finds themselves in debt, be they Leo or sensible Taurus, should deal with this as a matter of course and not 'consult their stars'.

It should also be said that some personality characteristics which may be a positive benefit in some situations can be a terrible hindrance in another. Typical Capricorns can be very paternal and directive. This could be regarded as good thing when someone is needing advice, solidity and reassurance, or a bad thing when the Capricorn becomes dictatorial, rigid and overbearing. The character tendency is the same: it is only the situation which is different.

Astrology can be beneficial, even if actual belief in its origins and methods is not understood, as it can get people to actually think about and consider themselves and others: how to form and maintain relationships, approach and confront character defects, and gain insight into how they and others work. This book should give valuable insights into astrology.

Air one of the four Elements. Air is associated with intellect, relationships and thought. The three Air signs are Gemini, Libra and Aquarius

Aquarius the Water Carrier (20 January–18 February). Eleventh sign of the zodiac. Fixed Air sign. Ruling planets: Saturn and Uranus

Aries the Ram (21 March–19 April). First sign of the zodiac. Cardinal Fire sign. Ruling Planet: Mars

ascendant sign also known as the Rising Sign. The sign of the zodiac which is on the eastern horizon at the time of birth. This sign is believed to show the general physical characteristics and personality of the person born at that time

astrology the study of the coincidence between the positions of the planets, the Sun and the Moon in relation to constellations of stars in the heavens with events on earth. It started as the study of the movement of planets and celestial bodies. The basis is that it is possible to suggest possible strengths, weaknesses and challenges associated with a person using this astrological information

birth chart a unique representation which shows the

positions of the Sun, Moon and planets in the zodiac signs and Houses at the time of birth of any individual. The date, time and place of birth need to be known as reference points. It is extremely unlikely, but not impossible, that two people would have the same birth chart

Cardinal one of the three Qualities. Cardinal is associated with beginnings, initiative and action. The Cardinal signs are Aries, Cancer, Libra and Capricorn

Cancer the Crab (21 June–22 July). Fourth sign of the zodiac. Cardinal Water sign. Ruling Planet: the Moon.

Capricorn the Sea goat (22 December–9 January). Tenth sign of the zodiac. Cardinal Earth sign. Ruling Planet: Saturn.

cusp the separation between the zodiac signs or Houses, or the start of each House

Earth one of the four Elements. Earth is associated with the here and now, reality and possessions. The three Earth signs are Taurus, Virgo and Capricorn

ecliptic the apparent path of the Sun around the Earth, although of course the Earth orbits the Sun

Element the Elements (Air, Earth, Fire and Water) are associated with general characteristics. See each individual Element for more information

equinox the time (in both spring and autumn) when the ecliptic crosses the Earth's equator. Day and night are the same length at the equinoxes. The spring, or vernal, equinox is around 21 March, while the autumn equinox is around 23 September

Fire one of the four Elements. Fire is associated with energy, transformation and enthusiasm. The three Fire signs are Aries, Leo and Sagittarius

Fixed one of the three Qualities. It is associated with preservation, solidity and determination. The four Fixed signs are Taurus, Leo, Scorpio and Aquarius

Gemini the Twins (21 May–20 June). Third sign of the zodiac. Mutable Air sign. Ruling Planet: Mercury

horoscope birth chart which is determined according to the exact time and place of birth

Houses used in compiling birth chart and correspond to the twelve zodiac signs. The position of each planet in the different Houses is the basis for the birth chart. Each House is concerned with an aspect of life. See the appendices for more information

Leo the Lion (23 July–22 August). Fifth sign of the zodiac. Fixed Fire sign. Ruling Planet: The Sun

Libra the Scales (23 September–22 October). Seventh sign of the zodiac. Cardinal Air sign. Ruling Planet: Venus

Mutable one of the three Qualities. It is associated with change, adaptability and harmony. The four Mutable signs are Gemini, Virgo, Sagittarius and Pisces

opposite signs the zodiac signs which are opposite each other on the zodiac wheel. The can either be opposing or complementary. They are as follows: Aries:Libra / Taurus:Scorpio / Gemini:Sagittarius / Cancer: Capricorn / Leo:Aquarius / Virgo: Pisces /

Libra:Aries / Scorpio:Taurus / Sagittarius:Gemini / Capricorn:Cancer / Aquarius:Leo / Pisces:Virgo

Pisces the Fishes (19 February–20 March). Twelfth sign of the zodiac. Mutable Water sign. Ruling Planets: Jupiter and Neptune

planets the eight major bodies in the heavens which orbit the Sun, except the Earth. These are the planets proper of Mercury, Venus, Mars, Jupiter, Saturn, Uranus, Neptune and Pluto. In astrology the Sun and Moon are also included. There is more information about the planets in the appendices

Quality behaviour associated with certain zodiac signs. There are three Qualities: Cardinal, Fixed and Mutable, roughly linked to the seasons: Cardinal signs (Aries, Cancer, Libra and Capricorn) begin the season; Fixed signs (Taurus, Leo, Scorpio and Aquarius) are in the middle of the season; while Mutable signs (Gemini, Virgo, Sagittarius and Pisces) fall in the period when the season is changing to the next

Rising Sign Also known as the Ascendant Sign. The sign of the zodiac which is on the eastern horizon at the time of birth. This sign is believed to show the general physical characteristics and personality of people born at that time

Ruling Planet each zodiac sign is thought to be especially influenced by one or more of the planets: Aries – Mars; Taurus – Venus; Gemini – Mercury; Cancer – the Moon; Leo – the Sun; Virgo – Mercury; Libra – Venus; Scorpio – Mars and Pluto;

Sagittarius – Jupiter; Capricorn – Saturn; Aquarius – Saturn and Uranus; Pisces – Jupiter and Neptune. There is more information about the Ruling Planets in the appendices

Sagittarius the Archer (22 November–21 December). Ninth sign of the zodiac. Mutable Fire sign. Ruling Planet: Jupiter

Scorpio the Scorpion (23 October–1 November). Eighth sign of the zodiac. Fixed Water sign. Ruling Planets: Mars and Pluto

solstice the time when the sun is furthest north or south from the Earth's equator. The summer solstice is around 21 June and the longest day of the year. The winter solstice, around 22 December, is the shortest

Star Sign commonly mistake for Sun Sign

Sun Sign the sign of the zodiac occupied by the Sun on the date of birth

Taurus the Bull (20 April–20 May). Second sign of the zodiac. Fixed Earth sign. Ruling Planet: Venus

Virgo the Virgin (23 August–22 September). Sixth sign of the zodiac. Mutable Earth sign. Ruling Planet: Mercury

Water one of the four Elements. It is associated with sensitivity, intuition and emotion. The three Water signs are Cancer, Scorpio and Pisces

zodiac an imaginary wheel, viewed as if from the centre of the solar system, and divided into twelve segments of 30 degrees. Each segment is named after a nearby constellation of stars

zodiac signs twelve 30-degree segments of the zodiac, reckoned anti clockwise according to their positions at the spring equinox. Aries is first, then Taurus, Gemini, Cancer, Leo, Virgo, Libra, Scorpio, Sagittarius, Capricorn, Aquarius, Pisces, which completes the revolution. This approximates to the constellations of stars into which the Sun has travelled at that time of year

zodiac wheel a representation of the zodiac. The wheel is divided into 30 degree segments and named after constellations of stars, the signs of the zodiac, in order. See zodiac signs above.

Aries

Taurus

Gemini

Cancer

Leo

Virgo

Libra

Scorpio

Sagittarius

Capricorn

Aquarius

Pisces

Aries

NAME	The Ram
DATES	21 March–19 April
RULING PLANET	Mars
ELEMENT	Fire
QUALITY	Cardinal
COLOUR	red
GEMSTONE	diamond and ruby
METAL	iron
ANIMAL	lamb and ram

Introduction and Background

Aries is the first sign of the zodiac, the Cardinal Fire sign. Although fire consumes, it also brings about change and transformation, sometimes extreme in nature, such as the smelting of iron from iron ore or aluminium from bauxite. As the Ram suggests, those typical of the sign of Aries have many characteristics believed to belong to that animal, such as determination, initiative, exploration, and daring, but also aggression, impetuousness, pigheadedness, a fiery temper, and a tendency to be reckless. Aries is also, as mentioned above, a Cardinal sign and the first in the spring season so is to do with new growth, energy and beginnings. Those influenced by the sign can be inspirational leaders, and their energy and creativeness can achieve much in many fields and many walks of life. As a frost in spring can damage or kill budding plants, those typical of Aries may start more than they finish. They have a tendency to find the beginning more interesting than the end.

In love and friendship those typical of Aries make good partners and companions, and get on especially well with the other Fire signs Sagittarius and Leo, as well as the Air signs Gemini, Aquarius and Libra: the latter sign is the opposite sign to Aries and such matches can be the best or worst of relationships. Aries can be more interested in the chase and conquest, but where there is enough energy, fire and interest in the partner, those typical of this sign can be excellent and loyal lovers or friends. Where interest is maintained, those under this sign will be content with a long-term commitment; however, Aries may also be happy with a string of meaningless but fiery relationships and conquests.

The symbol for Aries represents the ram's horns (or, it has also been suggested, the male genitalia). The small constellation of Aries, in the northern hemisphere, lies between Pisces and Taurus, and has one bright star. Ares was the Greek god of war, whose counterpart was Mars in Roman mythology.

Ruling Planet of Aries

The Ruling Planet of Aries is Mars, the Red Planet, and fourth in the solar system. It was known to the ancient, and Mars was the Roman god of war (Ares was his Greek counterpart), who was the father of Romulus and Remus. Those associated with the planet or where this planet is an influence may have much physical energy, and be bold and courageous. Mars is also associated with action, anger and desires. Mars, however, was hero to the underdog and an inspiration in battles of all kinds. Mars is the alchemical name for iron.

Characteristics of Aries

These are obviously general and can be modified by many factors, not least the influence of the Ascendant Sign and the different planets in different houses. Those typical of Aries who are frustrated or unhappy can exhibit some of the not so good characteristics, and of course a virtue in one situation, such as determination or passion, can be a vice in another. A passionate and faithful lover, in one set of circumstances, can be a dangerous and obsessed stalker in another. Those influenced by this sign do not like to be spurned, and can find it difficult to take no for an answer in love, work and life. They want to win, whatever the challenge, problem or game. They also believe that they are by far the most interesting person they know, and that they are better than those with whom they compete – even when it is obvious they are not.

Good Characteristics of Aries

- desires to lead and can be an inspired leader, manager or companion
- assertive, determined, enthusiastic and energetic: tends to get things done, no matter what obstacles are in the way
- daring and pioneering, and enjoys adventure and new challenges
- courageous, straightforward, honest and open: will rarely have a devious motive
- can be creative and passionate about their work
- often helps and protects others, particularly the vulnerable, the needy or the weak
- will do anything for loved ones and friends

Not So Good Characteristics of Aries

- desires to lead and hates being told what to do: does not like being second in command
- can enjoy new projects and experiences so much that things do not get finished if they become mundane or boring
- has to win, wants to be first, is overly competitive and must be in control of everything
- has a tendency to be aggressive and reckless, and to take needless risks, even where there are few or no benefits gained from doing so
- can be brash, inflexible, intolerant and take no heed or be simply unaware of other's feelings
- passionate, jealous and selfish: cannot see beyond their own needs

- can be too trusting and a poor judge of character: does not have the depth for insight into others' feelings

Appearance and Health of Aries

If someone has personality characteristics which are associated with Aries, they may also have the following physical traits:

- strong physically and energetic in mind and body
- wide shoulders, strong boned and long necked
- piercing and challenging eyes: others may feel threatened or that they are being challenged
- males may be bald while females have strong and luxuriant hair
- may have a scar from some physical fight which may be worn almost like a trophy
- walks with an air of confidence
- dresses appropriately to the situation

Those typical of Aries are usually healthy folk, and strive and fight off any illness which they chance to catch. When emotionally hurt or shocked by some unexpected event, however, they can be very vulnerable to sickness. Those typical of this sign may have little insight, even into their own health, especially if it is getting in the way of projects or experiences which interest them.

Fire signs are especially vulnerable to accidents and fevers, and Aries is no different, but they usually recover quickly. Illnesses which can be associated with the sign are neuralgia, headache, migraines, epilepsy and acne, as well as conditions of the sinuses, eyes and ears. Because of a certain recklessness and lack of care, accidents and mishaps are common, especially involving the head. When ill, however, typical Aries are poor patients and need constant reassurance and care, especially if they are physically or mentally incapacitated. Being an active sign, Aries hates to be bed-ridden and out of control: they may feel that their body has let them down, especially with a chronic condition which will not respond to treatment. Consequently, they may not give themselves long enough to recover, and may exacerbate illnesses and slow the healing process.

Parts of the body which are associated with Aries are the head and face including the eyes, ears, sinuses and brain, and sometimes also the bones and the blood. That is not to say that these parts of the body may be more susceptible to illness or particularly free from it. This strength or weakness can only be determined by doing a full birth chart.

Those under the sign rarely need rest during the day as they have abundant energy and enthusiasm. They can work late into the new morning, although they may find it difficult to get up in the morning and may prefer to rest late. Often a new project or activity is all that Aries requires rather than much rest or sleep. When undertaking less-interesting or mundane work, or where they cannot control a situation, those typical of this sign may feel very fatigued and frustrated.

Likes and Dislikes of Aries

Likes of Aries

- being liked and appreciated, especially for achievements
- meeting new people and new challenges
- good wine and food
- new clothes
- books and information
- bright flowers such as red roses
- disposable income

Dislikes of Aries

- being ignored or not getting appreciation
- coming second, third or fourth: has to be first in all things
- anyone or thing which is better at any activity or pursuit in which those typical of Aries are interested
- feeling hungry or thirsty or wanting for anything
- old or second-hand items
- being patient and waiting for things, especially when these are outwith their control
- uninteresting or unappetising food

Love Life and Friendship of Aries

Those with a strong Aries influence may be more interested in the chase and conquest, rather than settling down and making a home. Aries can be very attractive because of their high levels of energy, but they may not, especially the male, be very subtle in their pursuit, and their forwardness and lack of tact may make some uncomfortable and unresponsive. Those influenced by this sign can be deeply romantic and idealistic in love, doing all the right things and overcoming any obstacle. To some, however, it may be simply a means to go out with or sleep with a potential partner: they can be very goal driven.

The typical Aries can be extremely romantic and passionate although generally they like to do the chasing as they have a need to be in control. Being pursued themselves can be interesting but they may feel uncomfortable. Potential partners would do well to let those influenced by this sign believe they are in control. Aries can let others shine, though, and will not be put off by someone who is very special or talented, rather they will be supportive and appreciating provided their partner reciprocates.

The typical Aries can be very jealous of, and domineering with, their lover, especially if they think they are showing undue interest in someone else or are not putting Aries first. They may also be extremely possessive: some signs, especially Water and Earth, may find their burning passion rather too hot and seek a more relaxed and secure partner. Perversely, Aries will not understand a partner who is possessive in return, and can feel constricted in such a relationship.

Those influenced by the sign of Aries may also put their partner on a pedestal and almost worship them, which can be difficult to live up to and can lead to a mighty fall if the partner can not fulfil the expectations.

Those under this sign will, however, defend their partner through thick and thin, and stand by them in adversity. They also like a strong partner who can sustain their interest and keep the fires burning: weakness and a lack of energy do nothing for those influenced by this sign.

Aries expects complete faithfulness and to be loved above all others. They find criticism by partners extremely difficult to accept, and want their partner to treat them as if they were the first, and – of course – the best in love and sex.

Despite all this Aries can become bored and restless in a too comfortable or safe relationship. A relationship can burn itself out very quickly if there is no new fuel to keep it going, air to give it oxygen, or new challenges for those influenced by this sign. They enjoy the chase, and once the conquest has been achieved, may seek new adventures in pastures new. If this is not within the relationship, as they consider it is too dull or safe, then they may go outside it. Similarly Aries gets bored with routine in lovemaking and prefer variety and new experiences. Nevertheless, they will persevere at a relationship if they can see any hope that it will succeed or where they admire and respect their partner.

A partner who is regularly unfaithful, either sexually or emotionally, and deeply wounds the typical Aries will be hotly cast aside and even scorned. Those under this sign can be vindictive, especially when smarting from a hurt or when the sometimes fragile ego is bruised. This will tend to be done in an open angry way, and Aries can have a fiery and violent temper: bashing heads with anyone who has wounded or offended their pride.

In love and friendship, Aries does best with the other Fire signs Leo and especially Sagittarius. Sagittarians are also passionate and crave excitement so are a good match. Fire burns in Air, even needs it, so Aries can also form fine relationships with Libra, Gemini and Aquarius. Aries opposite sign is Libra: such friendship or relationships can be difficult, but can also be complementary and beneficial: Aries supplying energy and adventure, Libra constancy and balance, showing Aries how to cooperate with others and not just try to dominate them by force of personality. Often Aries needs to learn harmony and curb their aggression. However, there can also be too much friction, and the airy Libra and fiery Aries may just be too hot to hold and last.

Generally Aries does less well with Water and Earth signs, although Fire and Water produce steam, and Fire and Earth magma so such relationships may be explosive rather being stifling for those under Aries. Sometimes Aries does seek depth, security or stability, but more often they find these boring, and will soon be off on a new venture. Partners or friends from the Water and Earth signs may find those influenced by Aries fickle, unyielding and with a tendency to compete and domineer, which they may find irritating or unsatisfying.

Aries likes friends and partners who have some special skill or talent, and appreciates them in return for their own abilities. Those influenced by the sign like to have everyone thinking of them as their best friend: they do not like to be second in affection.

Often those under the sign, both women and men, prefer male company for friendship. Warmth and affection are offered by the typical Aries, but these friendships may not last long unless both remain interesting to the other. Despite often masking their insecurities with bravado, the ego of Aries may be very fragile and when threatened they can become aggressive, hostile and even nasty. Those influenced by this sign do enjoy company, as long as they can curb their competitiveness or socialise with others who appreciate the challenges they may provide.

Home Life of Aries

Those typical of Aries see home as somewhere to return after their adventures and conquests, a secure refuge in which to recuperate and plan before setting out on some new exploit. Alternatively, they see their home as somewhere to continue the exploration. As such those under this sign like to be the king of the castle, and to be masters in their home. Aries does not like to be tied down, and prefer to be the ones who decide what is the best procedure for executing home improvements or deciding on a new style of decoration. Those typical of this sign may be restless in a house which provides too little stimulation: Aries will rarely want to just rest and do nothing. They may want to entertain, and this they will do generously, although they may well want something in return from their guests. A social gathering may have some ulterior motive, even if it is just to receive praise for being a good and generous host.

When it comes to money, those typical of the sign of Aries may be somewhat extravagant and will see financial resources as a means to get on or get something they desire. They can be a bit thoughtless and impulsive when it comes to purchases, simply buying it because they take a whim rather than really wanting it or appreciating it once it is bought. They may also be generous with others, but this may be done mainly to impress. This need to be on top can lead them into trouble, unable to admit that they cannot afford something as they see this as an admission of failure.

As parents, those under this sign can attempt to rule or control their children, and may see disobedience as a battle of wills. This can lead to much conflict with offspring, especially as the children grown into teenagers and adulthood. Generally, the Aries parent will be deeply affectionate towards their offspring but will not coddle or spoil them. They will attempt to teach their youngsters how to win and be successful, and will do almost anything for them, being devoted to their children. As those under this sign are so competitive, they may transfer this to their children. Some typical of this sign may see their youngster being successful at sport or in an academic area as being more important than just loving their child for its own sake.

The typical Aries child also wants to be in charge, and is strong and usually quite active, both mentally and physically. They can have temper tantrums if they do not get their own way, although they will usually recover their good humour quickly. They also do not respond well to being told what to do in no uncertain terms, or even being cajoled or reasoned with. A more subtle approach – such as making chores into challenges for the Aries child to overcome – will probably prove more successful. A battle of wills will simply generate much anger and heat: the more the youngster feels it is being coerced, the more it will fight back.

Where there is both an Aries child and one or more parents who are typical of Aries, there may be trouble. Aries parents find it difficult not to try to control their offspring, and can be strict and unyielding disciplinarians. This approach is likely to cause many difficulties as the child grows up and particularly, as mentioned above, when they are in their rebellious teenage years.

The Aries child is usually warm and affectionate, and will want the same in return, especially if they have been hurt, either physically or emotionally. They can seem very confident and self-assured but, as all children, they are very vulnerable and their self-assurance may be just a mask of bravado. They will be generous and be pleased to let other children play with their toys. They will usually be happy to play alone as long as it is in a stimulating environment, but will also enjoy the company of other youngsters. They do have the tendency to bully or attempt to control their companions: it is difficult for them to let others take the lead.

The Aries youngster also has boundless enthusiasm and curiosity, but are prone to getting themselves into difficult or dangerous situations where they may get injured if not carefully supervised. Children typical of Aries will usually recover from injuries, fevers and childhood ailments very quickly. It should be said that those typical of this sign may not look after pocket money or savings well. It is probably good to try to teach them in childhood that there are times when they have to be careful, both in life and with their money.

Work Life of Aries

At work, those typical of Aries tend to like to lead rather than follow, and it is no surprise that if they have to answer to anyone at all it has to be the boss or owner of the enterprise rather than an under manager or second in command. Where work holds interest and advancement, those under this sign will work extremely hard and with considerable drive. They are not good with the mundane every-day running of a business, however, and are better at jobs which are creative or which need leadership – but where others will see to and concentrate on the fine detail.

Those typical of the sign will work extremely hard and as many hours as it takes, but will usually prefer to work late into the night than first thing in the morning. They do have complete belief in themselves, although this can be misplaced. Where this is warranted, they can turn around even ailing businesses. Generally, Aries is not good with money and should not do jobs which involve cost control and lots of paperwork.

Although they are usually loyal to the place they work, if those typical of Aries find their work boring, unrewarding or where their efforts are not appreciated, they will move and find somewhere new to make a living and where they feel they will get recognition for their efforts.

The working environment which will best suit an Aries is one where there is freedom of expression and movement, where the work is stimulating or challenging, where they can lead or initiate new projects – and where they are given recognition for their achievements. They will do less well where they need to blindly follow orders, where attention to detail is essential, or where they do not feel appreciated for the work they do.

Famous People with the Sun Sign Aries

Marlon Brando (actor), Casanova (lover),
Charlie Chaplin (actor), Joan Crawford (actor),
Doris Day (actor), Marcel Marceau (mime artist),
Eddie Murphy (actor and comedian),

Diana Ross (singer), Omar Sharif (actor),
Leonardo da Vinci (artist and inventor),
Tennessee Williams (writer).

Taurus

NAME	The Bull
DATES	20 April–20 May
RULING PLANET	Venus
ELEMENT	Earth
QUALITY	Fixed
COLOUR	blue, green
GEMSTONE	emerald and topaz
METAL	copper
ANIMAL	bull

Introduction and Background

Taurus is the second sign of the zodiac, and is the Fixed Earth sign. It is associated with the solid here and now, moving slowly but reliably towards a desired goal, and the practical here and now of any situation or environment. The typical Taurus is dependable and loyal, and often have a calm and considering nature. This is much like the Bull with which the sign is associated, although like that animal when angered, or on a charge, little can stop or deflect the rampaging Taurus. Material possessions and home life are very important, although those influenced by this sign may also be cautious to the point of inaction, even when a course of action is obvious and necessary. Taurus is a Fixed sign and the first in the spring season so is to do with consolidation and slow growth and building, less hasty but deeper and surer than the quick and primal Aries. Taurus can appear lazy, but often they are only taking time to make sure of the correct outcome: in the story f the tortoise and the hare, it is the tortoise who achieves its ambition and eventually completes the race.

In love and friendship, those typical of Taurus make good partners and companions, and get on especially well with the other Earth signs Capricorn and Virgo, as well as the Water signs Cancer, Pisces and Scorpio: the latter sign is the opposite sign to Taurus and such matches can be the best or worst of relationships. Taurus can be more interested in comfort and ease, but where there is enough stability, kindness and interest in the partner, those typical of this sign can be excellent and loyal lovers or friends. They are usually only interested in long-term relationships, and will rarely want a one-night stand.

The symbol for Taurus represents the bull's head with horns. Taurus is a constellation in the northern hemisphere, close to Orion, and between Aries and Gemini. It contains the crab nebula. Taurus is from the Latin for bull. The Minotaur of Crete, which roamed the labyrinth of Knossos, was part man, part bull.

Ruling Planet

The Ruling Planet of Taurus is Venus, second in the solar system, and often visible as a bright morning or evening star, when it can appear blue. It was known to the ancients, and Venus was the Roman god of love (Aphrodite was her Greek counterpart). Harmony, peace, beauty and art are associated with the planet, along with love and sensuality, of course. It is also associated with resources and possessions, and a comfortable home and life. Venus is the alchemical name for copper.

Characteristics of Taurus

These are obviously general and can be modified by many factors, not least the influence of the Rising Sign and the different planets in different Houses. Those typical of Taurus who are frustrated or unhappy can exhibit some of the not-so-good characteristics, and of course a virtue in one situation, such as patience or placidity, can be a vice in another. A dependable, patient and thorough worker is not so far from a stubborn, self-indulgent and obstructive lay about. Taurus can find it difficult to accept change, and can avoid taking any action at all without crippling and time-consuming consideration. They take the longer view and tend to only go forward with deep consideration because they believe the best is worth waiting for. However, when no obvious course presents itself, or where Taurus is feeling low or especially decisive, they may do nothing at all: ruminating at great leisure but to no purpose.

Good Characteristics of Taurus
- tends to be romantic, sentimental, earthy and sensual
- gentle, calm and placid: just the kind of person needed in a crisis
- craves and creates stability, even in shifting and uncertain situations
- appreciates prosperity, wealth and a comfortable home
- makes and keeps good friends and enjoys company and companionship
- concerned with nature, harmony, intuition and insight: can be very curious about many things, but especially those that improve understanding of themselves and their world
- can be very thorough, resourceful and tenacious: little can stop a bull once it has decided on a course of action
- dependable and attentive to friends and family
- values talents and abilities, both in the self and others
- usually well-organised with an attention to detail and manages time well

Not So Good Characteristics of Taurus
- can be self-indulgent and lazy: Taurus can enjoy

doing what appears to be, and may actually be, doing absolutely nothing

- possessive, both of people and things, and materialistic
- can be demanding of affection from friends and family
- inactive, stubborn and obstinate: little can move a bull if it does not want to be moved even when movement would be beneficial
- has a tendency to be shy and cautious, and can be easily embarrassed
- taciturn and can have little to say
- may appear to be dull and boring: something must be very interesting or it will just not hold the attention
- insensitive and may lack insight into the feelings of others: especially where they have already made up their minds
- not always a good judge of character
- takes too long considering and thinking about what to do
- inactive and conservative, letting life pass them by: they rarely grab the bull by the horns

Appearance and Health of Taurus

If someone has the personality characteristics which are associated with Taurus, they may also have the following physical traits:

- stocky, strong but compact body, sometimes with heavily muscled legs and especially thighs: they

may walk in a determined way which appears a bit
ponderous
- may have a tendency to be overweight or plump
- the shoulders may be wide and square, and the
neck somewhat short
- the face may be round in shape
- very good and clear complexion, and fine hair
- large or broad feet
- large eyes with a calm and steady gaze
- an air of mystery and hidden sensuality

Those influenced by Taurus are usually healthy
folk, and are pretty robust and strong, avoiding or
fighting off illness with ease because of their strong
constitutions. They may be overweight and somewhat
indolent, but will usually be fine and healthy unless
some extreme hurt or disturbance effects them. Taurus
can find it difficult to express anger or emotion, and do
not like change so they can remain situations which are
making them miserable. This can lead to frustration
and even depression, further compounded by the
knowledge that they should make some change but are
unwilling or unable to do so.

Those typical of Taurus often suffer from conditions
of the the throat, such as laryngitis, swollen glands and
croup. They may also get bouts of constipation. They
are, however, very stoic and can endure much pain and
discomfort: those influenced by Taurus hate to let
anything overcome them and will stubbornly fight off
illness. Taurus will also help any friend or family

member who suffers from any illness or other condition.

Parts of the body which are associated with Taurus are the throat and neck including the tonsils, thyroid gland and tongue, and sometimes also the kidneys, gonads and even the whole metabolic system. That is not to say that these parts of the body may be especially susceptible to illness or particularly free from it. This strength or weakness can only be determined by doing a full birth chart.

Taurus enjoys rest and leisure time, and is more than content to do absolutely nothing, as long as it is in comfortable surroundings and with good and relaxing friends. Holidays or weekends can be spent happily in front of the television or just chilling. Most people influenced by this sign find it easy to sleep well, although they do take some time to wake up and get going in the morning. Once they have finally arisen and got ready for the day, they do have lots of stamina and can work hard for long periods without becoming tired.

Likes and Dislikes of Taurus

Likes of Taurus
- quiet activities such as gardening, painting or listening to music
- having lots of money
- things which give some sort of sensual pleasure, such a food, drink or fine clothes
- eating fine food in good and sociable surroundings

- well ordered life where routine is set and all change is minimised
- good presents

Dislikes of Taurus
- any kind of change in routine or lifestyle
- being disturbed or bothered by people or events beyond their control
- lending things
- having to sleep in a strange bed: Taurus likes their own home
- being in a rush, either at home or at work
- not having enough time to consider, contemplate and work out their next move

Love Life and Friendships of Taurus

Those typical Taurus are very physical and romantic, but usually crave a long-term relationship rather than a one-night stand. They are usually devoted to their partner, and fall quickly into a steady match. Taurus loves beauty and glamour, but can be deceived by those wanting a quick fling or brief romance into believing that they have found the 'real thing'. They can also deceive themselves, even when they know a potential partner is completely unsuitable for their needs. When they are sure of a relationship, however, they will go for it wholeheartedly with no turning or looking back.

They love to be pampered and looked after, and enjoy physical contact such as cuddling and holdings hands. Taurus is also usually waiting for some commitment from their partner, as they like to feel secure and loved. Loyalty, gentleness and appreciation is a need for those influenced by this sign, and the typical Taurus will usually naturally fall into a routine, which needs to be accepted by any partner. In return they will be faithful, responsible and stable, and those wanting a satisfying long-term relationship will find it with those influenced by this sign. Taurus can, however, be somewhat possessive and prone to jealousy so that a partner should always make them feel special and appreciated. Birthdays, Christmas and anniversaries are very important and significant to Taurus, and cards and gifts should never be forgotten.

Those influenced by this sign tend to have a healthy attitude towards sex, and see it as a normal, natural and pleasurable experience. Taurus never uses sex as a weapon. They can, however, especially if female, be sensitive to being criticised about their physical appearance, although usually they are comfortable with nudity and their bodies.

Taurus may try and ignore any failings their partner may have, and may appear blind to their shortcomings, even when severe and obvious to others. The end of relationship is difficult as Taurus finds it difficult to admit that they chose the wrong person or that they were naive in trusting them – friends should also be careful not to interfere or try to influence the typical Taurus: no matter the situation. Having made up their minds that they are going to leave, they cannot then be deflected from their purpose. It can be difficult for them to acknowledge their feelings, denying hurt and pain both to others and to themselves. This may manifest itself in a series of illnesses which are difficult to diagnose as they slowly deal with their feelings of anger, disappointment or betrayal. Again friends should be wary of either saying 'I told you so' or in criticising ex-partners as it may anger the injured Taurus.

Those influenced by this sign, however, will never forgive an indiscretion or betrayal, no matter what the circumstances and no matter how apologetic or sorry their partner may be after the event. Taurus cannot forgive someone who has deeply wounded them, and the pain will stay with them for a very long time.

In friendship and love, Taurus does fine with the other Earth signs Virgo and Capricorn, although they are often attracted to the Water signs Cancer and Pisces, as well as Scorpio. Those typical of Taurus can find the best relationships with Scorpio, the Fixed Water sign of the zodiac, although they can be extremely difficult and tempestuous as well. Scorpio can help Taurus discover themselves, and understand the motives and drives of others as they see more deeply and more clearly. In return Taurus supplies solidity and a sensible down-to-earth approach which can ground the Scorpio. If the two signs can co-operate and complement this can produce an excellent match. If not, the relationship may be short lived and stormy.

Taurus is often attracted to or interested in the

more energetic signs such as Aries, Gemini or
Sagittarius, sometimes as a counterpoint to their own
inertia. However, they can become irritated or
impatient with these signs as Taurus prefers a more
settled and responsible partner or friend. Libra, an Air
sign, and Sagittarius, the Mutable Fire sign, can
produce much passion but also may prove the most
difficult of all. Taurus craves stability and security in
love in friendship, and the flighty Fire and ethereal Air
signs can often not provide this. However, boredom
can also be a factor when things are too safe, and
Taurus, or their partners or friends, may need stability
and security but also want excitement and novelty.
Those influenced by this sign can be a bit taciturn and
seem a bit dull to those without patience, but
underneath may crave freedom from their own
inaction.

Friendships will be long and enduring with those
the Taurus likes, and they are usually warm, gentle,
loyal and affectionate as friends. Those influenced by
this sign make the best relationships with those who
are reliable and have a common-sense approach to life,
and they do not like weakness, either mental or
physical, in their loved ones or those to whom they
feel close. Good taste and those with some skill, talent
or power are particularly appreciated, as are those who
persevere and show endurance. The typical Taurus
does not like ostentation or pretence, although the
genuine article can impress.

Home Life of Taurus

Those typical of Taurus view relaxation and comfort as very high in their priorities, and consequently will create a secure and pleasant home. This will be free from stress as far as is possible, and as they can spend much of their time resting and taking it easy, they will create a tranquil environment free from worry and strain. Taurus hates change, and especially dislike things being moved around. Once the furniture or decor in a room has been chosen, they will rarely be changed: even the furniture will be left as it is. The house will be well organised and those typical of Taurus will fall into patterns when cleaning, cooking or doing other household chores – not that these are usually very high up the priorities. Those typical of this sign like precious, tasteful or artistic possessions, such as paintings, sculpture and books, and may even actively collect such items. They will also want to own their own home rather than to rent or share.

Those typical of the sign of Taurus tend to be very careful and acquisitive with their money and material belongings. More than any other sign, Taurus is interested in the here and now, yet they will rarely ever get into debt unless absolutely necessary. They may have the tendency to hoard their wealth just for the sake of it, and to other more generous signs they may seem mean. Taurus will always employ their wealth to good effect, and will always buy tasteful and well-made goods – which will be even more highly regarded and sought after if there is a chance they will accumulate in value.

As parents Taurus is affectionate and loving, and has endless patience and care for their youngsters. They will always try to do the best for their child, and will nurture them and encourage them. Those typical of this sign can be a little domineering with their offspring, and also expect a lot from them. Taurus always thinks about the future, and will usually save to make sure that the offspring can be well cared for.

The typical Taurus child is normally quiet and placid, and will rarely have tantrums or outbursts of emotion. Indeed, they can be very quiet. Although they are usually very physical and like to be cuddled and hugged, they hate being the centre of attention or being forced to perform in public. Taurus is usually shy when it comes to making outward shows.

They can be incredibly stubborn and unmovable, however, when they have decided what they want, and they will always try to assert themselves quietly but implacably. Similarly, if a parent tries to force them to do something they do not want to do, they will hold their ground, no matter what punishments are threatened. Taurus children are more likely to respond to reasoned argument, especially where this is backed up with common sense, or by being shown affection and love as a means of changing their mind. They do not necessary like to play with other children, and many will be content just to be left to their own devices. Taurus may seem a little slow at school, but they are usually well organised and will work steadily until they catch up or even overtake their contemporaries. Once something has been learned, they rarely forget it.

Taurus can be quiet and placid on the surface, but this can mask a range of very deep emotions going on below, that they just do not want to reveal. It may be beneficial to help children typical of this sign to show at least some of these feelings and to express and assert themselves in other ways apart from being obstinate, implacable or silent. It is very important that the Taurus child gets lots of attention and affection, but it is also vital that they are not smothered. They will thrive in a tranquil and pleasant environment which is free from conflict and stress. They respond to beauty and peace, and will enjoy music and art, in which they are more often than not very talented. However, as mentioned above, they do not like to be the centre of attention, even if it is to praise them for their achievements. This does not mean that Taurus is shy or retiring, only that they want to be left in peace or do not see the need to be in the limelight.

If a Taurus child has a Taurus parent this can be difficult as one can be as immovably obstinate as the other. This can lead to long periods of quiet conflict as the two battle for supremacy. The Taurus parent would do well to employ the tactics as mentioned above as, although they may be unmovable themselves, the Taurus youngster is even more obstinate and difficult to coerce.

Work Life of Taurus

At work, those typical of Taurus are good, thorough and dedicated workers, and perform particularly well in a practical and down-to-earth work environment. They will do even better where the surroundings are peaceful and well-ordered: Taurus does not like to have to work in a tense or hostile atmosphere. They also do not like people who interfere with their work, and they prefer to be given enough time to consider and make the right choices. In a rushed or pressurised business, they may respond well to emergencies and 'fire fighting' as they can remain calm when all around them are losing their heads, but they will always desire a more relaxed and sensible way of working. To the Taurus, leaving everything until the last moment is simply not sensible, desirable or the way to get work done well.

They may seem slow and even ponderous to other more hasty signs, but they will always work steadily and get the job done on time – no matter what obstacles may lie in the way. Taurus is especially good with money as they are careful and sensible, but they also like a regular income in secure employment: they may not be the right people to be self-employed if there is any risk involved. Those typical of this sign will always give colleagues the benefit of the doubt, but if they feel betrayed or let down, they will never forgive the person, even if they never actually say anything to that effect.

Those typical of Taurus are excellent workers when

they are given time to complete work at their own pace, and where being calm and solid is an advantage. They do less well where they are expected to take executive action, where they are given too little time, and where the workplace is always pressurised and there is conflict between colleagues or customers.

Famous People with the Sun Sign Taurus

Candice Bergen (actor), Cher (singer and actor), Judy Collins (writer), Duke Ellington (musician), Ella Fitzgerald (singer), Henry Fonda (actor), Sigmund Freud (psychologist), Jack Nicholson (actor), Michelle Pfeiffer (actor), William Shakespeare (playwright and writer),
Barbra Streisand (singer and actress),
Queen Elizabeth (monarch of Britain).

Gemini

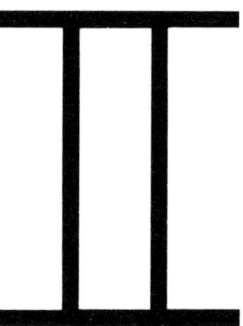

NAME	The Twins
DATES	21 May-20 June
RULING PLANET	Mercury
ELEMENT	Air
QUALITY	Mutable
COLOUR	yellow
GEMSTONE	agate, garnet
METAL	mercury
ANIMAL	magpie

Introduction and Background

Gemini is the third sign, and the Mutable Air sign of the zodiac, and is associated with the communication, the creation of harmony, and adaption as needs are identified but alter over time. As the Twins suggest, this sign is to do with relationships with other people, home, work and the world; and the relationship with the self: two halves which form a whole. These can sometimes be either complementary or in opposition, and can also represent either peace or warring within the self. Gemini is changeable and adaptable, and often has a liberal and charming nature, especially enjoying talking and entertaining. Those typical of this sign can get bored with the mundane or routine, and this may result in fickleness and irritability, and an inability to see things through. Gemini is a Mutable sign and the first in the spring season so is to do with transition, the end of the spring changing into the beginning of summer.

In love and friendship, those typical of Gemini make good partners and companions, and get on especially well with the other Air signs Libra and Aquarius, as well as the Fire signs Aries, Leo and Sagittarius: the latter sign is the opposite sign to Gemini and such matches can be the best or worst of relationships. Gemini can be somewhat restless, fickle and unwilling to commit, but where there is enough harmony with, and interest in, the partner, those typical of this sign can be excellent and loyal lovers or friends. Where the partner is the 'other half', the true twin of those under this sign, the Gemini will be happy with a long-term commitment; however, Gemini may have a string of unsatisfactory relationships while they search for the ideal partner. Often the relationship can be with the self as much as with another.

The symbol for Gemini is the Roman numeral for 'two', for the twins, the origin being the mythical Castor and Pollux, twins (although they had different fathers) who chose to be united in the sky as a constellation rather than ever to be separated. Gemini is a constellation in the northern hemisphere, between Taurus and Cancer, and contains the stars Castor and Pollux, the two brightest in the constellation.

Ruling Planet

The Ruling Planet of Gemini is Mercury, first in the solar system, as well as being the smallest and nearest to the sun. It was known to the Romans, and Mercury was the messenger of Jupiter and the gods (Hermes was his Greek counterpart). The planet is associated with communication, thought, intelligence and mental activities. The metal mercury, which is also known as quicksilver, is a heavy silvery liquid at room temperature.

Characteristics of Gemini

These are obviously general and can be modified by many factors, not least the influence of the Ascendant Sign and the different planets in different Houses. Those typical of Gemini who are frustrated or unhappy can exhibit some of the not-so-good characteristics, and of course a virtue in one situation, such as light-footedness and not being reliant on others, can be a vice in another. Being quick, versatile and inventive is not so far from being impractical, impatient and restless. Gemini can find it difficult to settle down or commit to any long-term project, work, home or love. They can also be changeable to the point of being vaporous, and as a Mutable sign can be virtually impossible to pin down.

Good Characteristics of Gemini
- communicative and articulate: can persuade others to do what is wanted with ease
- can and gets much enjoyment from doing two or more things at once
- loves to learn new things and finds quizzes and puzzles fascinating
- tends to be charming, entertaining and amusing
- can be quick, lively, versatile, nimble and dexterous
- inventive, curious and like to explore new areas (although sometimes only for short periods!)
- concerned with intellect and intuition
- liberal and broad-minded, being able to see both points of view in arguments
- very resourceful and adaptable to a variety of situations

Not So Good Characteristics of Gemini
- restless, flighty and easily bored, especially when sustained concentration is needed on tasks or aspects of life which they find mundane
- impractical and unrealistic: can expect too much from the world, other people, and the self
- fickle, changes opinion without reason, and unreliable
- finds it difficult to settle down or commit to anything
- can enjoy a good gossip, can be sarcastic,

sometimes malicious, and likes to stir things up
- manipulative and devious, albeit often with great charm and subtlety
- does not know when to stop
- may have a dual personality, may be at war with the self, and tends to be inconsistent: often in 'two minds'

Appearance and Health of Gemini

If someone has personality characteristics which are associated with Gemini, they may also have the following physical traits:
- tall in stature than average and upright in posture
- darting eyes which do not apparently concentrate on anything in particular for long
- rough complexion with a tendency to become pock-marked
- often look younger than they actually are
- quick, strong, agile and active
- long limbs
- fleshy hands

Those typical of Gemini are usually healthy folk, especially when they have plenty of space and air: they may be come ill if stifled or suffocated in work, relationships or home life. Conflicts can also arise from within the self. Those influenced by this sign also find it difficult to discover ways to relax and are prone to nervous exhaustion. Gemini can also find it difficult to make decisions, even about health and well being – or what is the right course of action or treatment.

Illnesses associated with Gemini include coughs and colds as well as other chest conditions. They also may be vulnerable to speech problems. The ill Gemini tends to hide their suffering, and will get irritated by anyone asking how they are, no matter how sympathetic and well meaning that person might actually be. They especially hate being incapacitated or bed ridden, and will be restless even when seriously ill.

Parts of the body which are associated with Gemini are the fingers, hands, arms, shoulders and lungs, and sometimes also the nervous system and speech organs. That is not to say that these parts of the body may be especially susceptible to illness or particularly free from it. This strength or weakness can only be determined by doing a full birth chart.

The typical Gemini, as mentioned above, finds it virtually impossible to rest or relax, even when it would be beneficial. Even when apparently doing nothing, those under this sign will be thinking and considering ten to the dozen. Leisure time and holidays need to be spent doing something as relaxing as possible without being boring, activities which occupy the mind without taxing the body or spirit.

Likes and Dislikes of Gemini

Likes of Gemini
- having plenty of room to explore and move about in
- travelling and the excitement from the anticipation

of travel
- being with friends, family or even acquaintances: people are very important
- learning, knowledge and information, especially when about to tell others
- anything new or novel
- playing devil's advocate in discussions and arguments
- chatting, telephone, faxes and email: any way of communicating quickly
- unravelling a puzzle

Dislikes of Gemini
- enforced routine, making commitments and fixed ideas
- not being able to escape a mundane endless task
- having to wait for anything
- wasting time which could be better spent
- being kept in the dark or information being withheld from them
- losing at anything, no matter how important or trivial

Love Life and Friendships of Gemini

Those which are strongly influenced by the zodiacal sign of Gemini are often looking for an ideal and romantic relationship, which they may believe can only be truly realised with their soul mate. Gemini may search for many years for the perfect partner, and may have numerous relationships and flings of varying intensity and length until they succeed. Part of the challenge may be that they are not sure what they are wanting. Indeed, this may change over time anyway. Even when they think they have found the dream partner, they then realise this is not who they want. They may have been searching for an idealised fantasy figure which simply does not exist in the real world. If they can find their ideal partner, however, the match can be joyous and completely fulfilling. The two halves of the relationship are joined, and the Gemini feels whole.

The typical Gemini is extremely romantic underneath, although they will probably have had many relationships and even entanglements. Those influenced by this sign can become quite cynical and pessimistic about finding true love, while others have expectations which are unrealistic and unachievable. Gemini is not always good at forming lasting or deep relationships. Their fickleness can also come into play or it may take some time for it to become apparent that their partner may not be the one for whom they have been searching. Despite all this, they are usually witty, good company, warm and charming, and they will show genuine interest in someone who has anything to offer.

In a relationship the Gemini can be confused and unable to cope with their emotions, especially when at loggerheads with their normally considering side. If they feel deep passion with their hearts, but remain uncertain in their heads, there can be a deep conflict within the self. To their lover or potential partner, they may seem cool and distant, and never show their true feelings, which can lead to much frustration. Gemini can feel very deeply, despite their airy nature, and may become very needy and dependent, requiring constant reassurance. They also, however, need a partner they view as equal in every way.

Those under this sign believe that their ideal partner should understand them completely, almost know and predict their every move and action. They are looking for complete loyalty and faithfulness, although they want this is an open and free environment. Gemini does not want to restrict a partner or curtail their lives, nor do they themselves want constriction: rather they want both themselves and their partner to grow together in a spacious relationship where they have freedom to move and flourish. Tenderness and empathy is necessary to those influenced by this sign, and they will show warmth and generosity in return. Gemini does enjoy flirting, as well as talking and communicating, and will not get on with the taciturn or shy.

Gemini will often use sex to release the build up of pent-up emotion or frustration. This may mean an intense burst of activity, which may quite quickly subside as those influenced by this sign get their emotional needs met. Companionship and company are as important as sex, and the quality of the emotional relationship itself, of which the physical is obviously a component, is vital.

Maintaining interest is important to Gemini, and if a relationship stagnates or becomes too boring or safe, those influenced by this sign will move on. They also find it difficult to manage when their partner is needy and demanding: many just do not have the resources to nourish another without getting nourishment back in return.

Although the decision will always have been carefully considered, the end of relationship may appear to come quite suddenly: the ex-partner will be left in no doubt. The Gemini may be off without a backward glance. If the partner, however, breaks off the relationship, especially when they have been especially cherished, this can leave those under this sign bewildered and wounded, albeit often for just a short time. This can manifest itself either in appearing aloof and cool, or may result in a burst of deep anger. Either way, the Gemini will normally move quickly on, and resume the quest to find the perfect partner – or at least someone to keep them occupied in the meantime.

In love and friendship, those under the sign of Gemini form the best matches with the other Air signs Libra and Aquarius, as well as Gemini. These signs are particularly compatible as they understand each other's needs. Gemini also does well with the Fire signs Aries, Leo and particularly with Sagittarius, as air and fire combust and burn together, provided there is enough air for Fire and enough kindling for Air. Gemini can form the best relationships with Sagittarius, the Mutable Fire sign, as those influenced by Sagittarius have a more ordered and focused approach to love and the world. If the two signs can complement each other then it will work well; alternatively if they cannot get on this may be a brief and fiery relationship. Virgo, at least in some circumstances, is another compatible sign as they have the same Quality and Ruling Planet, but also supply some challenges which benefit both signs. Again this can also be the most unsatisfactory of relationships.

Friendships can be enduring with Gemini as long as the friend or partner shows a lively interest in the world, is prepared to try out new pastimes, and enjoys conversation and a bit of a gossip. Those influenced by Gemini are genuinely interested in others, and will always be ready and willing to help should some sudden emergency arise. They are also warm and witty, and usually very good company, whatever the situation.

They do, however, enjoy stories and gossip, and like to embellish their tales to make them more interesting. This may leave little of the truth: Gemini never let the facts get in the way of a good story. Because they can also leave everything to the last minute, they may be late for appointments or meetings, and they like to be spontaneous: they may find those who are more studied or considering boring and unrewarding. Those typical of Gemini like to keep in touch and know all the latest news, and therefore like to be contacted by letter, email, fax or phone. They may find it difficult to forgive a friend who kept something from them or informed others without telling Gemini.

Home Life of Gemini

Those typical of the zodiac sign of Gemini are not usually great home makers, and see the place they stay as just a staging point on their great journey through life. They will prefer somewhere where they have plenty of room in which to move about, both physically and emotionally: Gemini will not want their home to tie them down or constrict them. Nevertheless, their home will be a place full of interest, bright and lively, and filled with the many mementos of their travels.

As they hate to be out of touch, those typical of this sign will have many ways of keeping abreast of things, both communicating with friends and keeping up to date with news and the latest information. A telephone, at least, is essential, and a computer with email and access to the world wide web will also be wanted. Gemini will also feel more secure with some means of transport nearby, so that they can get off quickly without any fuss or delay, even if they never actually use it. They will also have as many people around to their home as possible, as they love to entertain and meet new people and old friends alike: those under this sign hate to feel lonely or alone.

When it comes to money, those under the sign of Gemini hardly give it a second thought. Material wealth and possessions are not of great interest to a

Gemini, except where a lack may actually be constricting and restrict their freedom and ability to travel about and communicate. Consequently, Gemini may have huge bills and not even be aware of it, or care much, until the phone is cut off or the computer with their email is repossessed. As long as nothing is said or done, the Gemini will be happy to run up absolutely massive debts and will continue to increase their commitments no matter how unable they are to cover them.

As parents, Gemini are very able as they are so adaptable, and they quickly understand the wants and needs of their child. They love to impart information and will enjoy teaching and playing with their offspring. They will, however, try to reason and get over the point with logic, even when dealing with a difficult, obstinate or badly behaved child: which may not always be very successful. Those typical of this sign can also have trouble with any strong emotions, including love for their child, and may hide how they feel or find the strength of their feelings quite troubling.

The typical Gemini child is very bright and friendly, and loves to talk and interact with other children, adults and the world in general. They may sometimes seem a little distracted, as if they are in two minds about everything or are away in a fantasy world of their own. This latter state can often happen if the environment they are in is too mundane, monotonous or dull for their inquisitive and lively nature.

Youngsters influenced by Gemini can pick up things very quickly, will usually learn to read without any trouble, and will be very dexterous and skilled for a child. They may seem somewhat precocious, and will need lots of stimulation and space. If they feel constricted or are bored, they will be very grumpy and irritable, or may become detached and retreat to live in the more ethereal world of their imagination.

Special care is needed with children who are typical of Gemini. As they are so adventurous and inquisitive, and learn so quickly, they can get themselves into dangerous situations if not carefully supervised. This supervision, however, should not be by stopping them exploring, but they will need taught to distinguish between what is safe and what is dangerous, which perils are real and which are imaginary.

Gemini youngsters will also need lots of friends of both sexes to keep them happy, although they may never show who they actually like. They want to be understood and accepted, and will have many and varied interests and hobbies. These hobbies may not hold the interest for long, and this restlessness is something that the parent should tackle if possible: often those under this sign take too little time or do not have enough determination, even on projects or areas which could interest them.

A Gemini parent with a Gemini child will usually understand each other well, but the parent may find it difficult to set rules as if they often do not see the point of them. The parent needs to ground the young Gemini and one challenge can be teaching them determination and thoroughness as often the parent does not possess these themselves.

Work Life of Gemini

Those influenced by Gemini are very good workers, and will usually achieve whatever they set out to do provided it holds their interest. They are very friendly, charming and companionable, and will prefer a workplace where they can chat and joke with colleagues. As a rule, those typical of this sign do not like petty rules or tasks which are boring or mundane. They may cut corners, become irritable and impatient, or simply not complete this kind of business. They are, however, good at sorting out problems or dealing with unforeseen emergencies, as well as analysing and appraising projects or areas of work. This is especially important if dealing with people or a project which needs good communication.

Gemini may not work well if they feel they are tied to the office: if meeting customers or contractors, they may be more effective if they meet them off-site, either at their own places of work or somewhere to where the Gemini can travel. Those typical of Gemini are not necessarily very good with money and cost control as they are far more concerned with communication than expense.

Those typical of this sign do not have fixed ideas about anything, and so are excellent at managing radically new projects or areas. They are also good at work where they can be allowed to delegate, and can be especially effective if they have a colleague who is good at detail and form filling. As mentioned above, a constricting or rigid work environment will simply not get the best from a Gemini: they need air and space to explore and to meet new and interesting people and challenges.

Gemini is an excellent communicator and investigator and will enjoy jobs in the media or where they can bring their inquisitive intellect to bear. Where a workplace is overly disciplined or rigid, or where work is mundane and dull, those typical of this sign will do less well.

Famous People with the Sun Sign Gemini

George Bush (politician), Miles Davies (musician), Bob Dylan (musician), Clint Eastwood (actor), Judy Garland (actor and singer), Bob Hope (comedian and actor), Paul McCartney (musician and singer), Marilyn Monroe (actor), Queen Victoria (monarch of Britain).

Cancer

NAME	The Crab
DATES	21 June-22 July
RULING PLANET	Moon
ELEMENT	Water
QUALITY	Cardinal
COLOUR	silver, yellow-orange, indigo
GEMSTONE	pearl, amber, moonstone
METAL	silver
ANIMAL	crab, turtle, sphinx

Introduction and Background

Cancer is the fourth sign of the zodiac, and the Cardinal Water sign. It is associated with security, nurturing and deep feelings. The Crab has a hard shell, into which the Cancer retreats when threatened or as protection against the world. Those typical of Cancer often see their home or some other place as a sanctuary, like the inside of the crab's shell. Those influenced this sign can also be crabby or nippy: the

Crab not only has its hard shell but also pincers which can give a nasty wound. Crabs also move sideways, but ultimately get where they desire: the typical Cancer can be subtle and sensible, or even manipulative and cunning, yet often achieve what they desire without being noticed by others. This sign is also often seen as being maternal, and is associated with family and nurturing (the 'paternal' sign of the zodiac is usually thought of as being Capricorn). Cancer is also a Cardinal sign and the first in the summer season so is to do with nurturing and growth, the beginning of summer.

In love and friendship those typical of Cancer make good partners and companions, and get on especially well with the other Water signs Pisces and Scorpio, as well as the Earth signs Taurus, Virgo and Capricorn: the latter sign is the opposite sign to Cancer and such matches can be the best or worst of relationships. Cancer can be rather unsure of themselves and too easily hurt so unwilling to get involved, but where there is enough security, overt affection and interest in the partner, those typical of this sign can be excellent and loyal lovers or friends. Where the partner can bring the Cancer out of their shell those under this sign will be happy with a long-term commitment; however, Cancer may find it difficult to take the first step and may retreat from anything which can hurt them.

The symbol for Cancer is a rotated '69', for the crab, and it has also been associated with two turtles as recorded in Egyptian mythology. The myth behind Cancer the Crab is from Greek mythology when Juno, Jupiter's wife, placed the constellation in the sky as a reward for helping slow down one of the labours of Hercules: the poor crab was squashed in the process. Cancer is a small and faint constellation in the northern hemisphere, between Gemini and Leo.

Ruling Planet

The Ruling Planet of the sign of Cancer is the Moon, the satellite of the Earth. The planet is associated with emotions and instincts, as well as the unconscious and memory. The Moon waxes and wanes, and this is reflected by the changing moods of those associated with the Moon, from elation to depression, then back again. The Moon is also extremely powerful, nothing can stop it from producing the spring and neep tides on Earth, from the force of its gravity.

Characteristics of Cancer

These are obviously general and can be modified by many factors, not least the influence of the Ascendant Sign and the different planets in different Houses. Those typical of Cancer who are frustrated or unhappy can exhibit some of the not-so-good characteristics, and of course a virtue in one situation, such as being self-sacrificing and dependable, can be a vice in another. Being loving, devoted and protective is not so far from being moody, over-sensitive and smothering. Cancer can find it difficult to manage in any insecure environment: be it work, home or love. They can also become overly concerned with dreams and the occult, their interest or even obsession terrifying them more and more. They can also be the most passive-aggressive of zodiac signs, never openly attacking someone but nipping away in the background.

Good Characteristics of Cancer

- receptive, shrewd and intuitive: will often see others' motives, drives and ambitions
- may be kind, compassionate, adaptable and nurturing
- often associated with motherhood and mothering: as above, Cancer is very maternal
- can be tenacious and determined if a goal is desired: will hold on until they succeed
- has a good memory and is often interested in history and family
- makes good friends and will usually keep in touch over many years
- concerned with intellect and intuition: will often have interests in art, music and literature
- often interested in dreams, the occult and psychic ability
- concerned with home building, comfortable surroundings and domesticated: the home is very important
- sensible with money and in financial matters

Not So Good Characteristics of Cancer

- possessive, vulnerable, clinging (with those pincers!) and too easily hurt: when wounded they will retreat into somewhere secure and from there man the barricades
- good memory so tends to remember and nurture perceived insults or snubs for all time
- moody: may be happy and relaxed one minute, depressed and despairing the next
- sentimental and nostalgic: a tendency to believe that times in the past can not be bettered; that the future holds nothing but uncertainty and trouble
- overpowering in intensity and may smother friends and family, especially if trying to mother them
- may be selfish and overly self-interested
- crabby and nippy in nature
- manipulative, potentially sneaky, and difficult to pin down
- introspective and can become obsessed with indefinable fears, even the occult and the supernatural
- tendency to become depressed if not surrounded by family and friends, there are problems or friction at work, or the home is not comfortable or secure
- can influence friends and family, either making them happy and contented, or sad and restless

Appearance and Health of Cancer

If someone has personality characteristics which are associated with Cancer, they may also have the

following physical traits:
- very expressive and strong features, which reflect every emotion however fleeting
- moon-shaped and pale face with soft skin
- alternatively may have a large head, somewhat crab-like in appearance with high cheekbones and obvious brows
- a combination of the two above facial types
- has a tendency to be overweight and can put on weight easily
- larger chest than hips, and may be quite broad shouldered
- small and chubby or large and long hands and feet

Those typical of Cancer are usually healthy people, and provided they have security and lots of people around them to give them attention and affection they will thrive and happily scuttle about. Problems can arise when they become anxious or lonely, and their health can suffer from anxiety and depression. If they feel unloved or lonely for long periods then they can be especially vulnerable.

Conditions associated with the sign can be centred on the stomach and the upper gastrointestinal tract including indigestion and eating disorders. Other problems can be coughs and illnesses which produce catarrh, as well as anaemia and fatigue. Those influenced by the sign may also have a tendency to suffer from severe depression. Some influenced by Cancer can become complainers almost by habit, but others will not talk about an illness until it has become very serious: either emotional, mental or physical. Sometimes a condition or problem is so serious that they cannot confront it.

Parts of the body which are associated with Cancer are the breasts and stomach, including the ribs, oesophagus, upper gastrointestinal tract, gallbladder and sometimes also the womb. That is not to say that these parts of the body may be especially susceptible to illness or particularly free from it. This strength or weakness can only be determined by doing a full birth chart.

Cancer finds it easy to rest when in comfortable and secure environments surrounded by attentive people with whom they feel affection and trust. Those influenced by the sign do relax by doing very little, but they need their emotional needs met or their health and well-being will suffer.

Likes and Dislikes of Cancer

Likes of Cancer
- their mother and anyone who loves their own mother: they also like to mother their own friends
- comfortable and secure home
- stories about friends and family, and genealogy and family history
- shopping and purchasing gifts
- fine food and drink
- being in company with cherished friends and family
- being complimented or shown affection

- physical contact
- tranquil workplace without friction or tension

Dislikes of Cancer
- being involved in a crisis, particularly if it is their responsibility to sort it out
- having their home or cooking criticised, in however minor a way
- being forced to take part in discussions or conversations when they do not wish to do so
- being questioned about health or problems
- those who forget birthdays or Christmas, or names and dates, especially when this relates to family or friends

Love Life and Friendship of Cancer

Those influenced by the sign of Cancer are very physical, and see love and sex as two sides of the same coin. Cancer is concerned with a comfortable home and security, and will thrive when this is combined with a steady stream of warmth and affection. Those typical of Cancer often need to be coaxed from their shell, but where this is successful and sincere they will make a very fulfilling and satisfying relationship. Those under this sign are very romantic, and appreciate time and effort being spent on them.

Cancer can be very subtle in their pursuit of a potential partner, but will rarely be seen to make the first move. They can give out very mixed messages, one time seeming cold and unresponsive, another friendly and warm. For all this, they will often get what they want, and if they think someone is interested in them they will stay interested themselves. Some of this reluctance to be seen to be making a move is because of the Cancer fear of rejection and of showing their true selves: inside they are very soft and they find pain unbearable. Partners or potential partners should be careful not to criticise Cancer, especially near the beginning of a relationship, as this will drive those influenced by Cancer back into their shells, where they will feel deeply hurt and may not emerge again.

Cancer puts their loved ones above everyone and everything else, and they can be completely devoted and loyal to their partner. This they need in return. They can, however, be clingy and demanding, and they may attach themselves with an iron grip, making it impossible to be shaken off: they like to dominate their partner. Some may find their persistence and tenaciousness attractive, while others will find this difficult to cope with: this kind of person would do better to fine someone not influenced by Cancer.

Cancer is also changeable, and their moods can alter quickly and without warning. The harder the ex-partner tries to leave the Cancer, the harder and more determined the Cancer is to hold on. Those who desire a brief or meaningless relationship should be aware that the typical Cancer may believe there is more going on: often those influenced by Cancer are looking for commitment.

The typical Cancer is often seen as maternal, hard

working and sensible, and will try to bring income into their home and increase financial security. Those influenced by this sign are interested in family and children, and will usually want offspring.

They find it difficult to admit that a relationship is over, especially the more they are emotionally attached. They can find it difficult to differentiate between true love and emotional hunger. This is exacerbated during an unsatisfying relationship: the less love and attention shown to the Cancer, the more they demand and require. If a partner is not strong enough to provide this, those under this sign may drain them all of energy. This makes it both impossible to continue with the relationship, but also very difficult to finish it. Alternatively, those influenced by this sign may simply scuttle off and find someone new who can provide what they need.

Cancer can act quite aggressively and vindictively if betrayed by an unfaithful partner. They can become increasingly jealous, and increasingly determined to exact some revenge. Those intending to be unfaithful should bear this in mind: the pincers of the crab can inflict a painful and messy wound.

In friendship and love, those influenced by Cancer form good matches with the other Water signs Scorpio and Pisces, as well as the Earth signs Taurus, Virgo, and Capricorn. Water keeps earth damp and fruitful, allowing growth and nurturing. Those influenced by Cancer can find the best relationships with Capricorn as the Cardinal Earth sign. Capricorn is seen as being paternal, and therefore complementary and opposite to Cancer, which is seen as maternal. Capricorn can help Cancer improve their judgment and to get things more into perspective, bringing the crab from their shell into a caring but firm environment. If the two signs can get on, this can produce a fulfilling relationship for both parties. If not, this can end in a muddy mess.

Generally, Cancer does not do well with the Fire signs as water extinguishes fire or heats it to boiling point, producing steam but little else. There may be some attraction between Cancer and fun-loving Leo, as long as Leo gets the attention and then reciprocates, giving Cancer love and attention in return: yet often this reciprocation does not happen. Gemini, the Mutable Air sign, and Cancer can also form interesting relationships, but Gemini can become quickly smothered.

Friendships will be long and satisfying as long as friends are generous with their emotions and their money: generally, Cancer will give more in return. Those influenced by the sign look after their friends like valued possessions, and try to nurture them. They do, however, have long memories, and if they feel hurt or betrayed they will nurse their anger. With old friends, there may be reconciliations, while new friends are quickly abandoned. Those typical of Cancer do not like to reveal much of themselves, and a friend will often be the last person to know that something has gone wrong or that they are hurting inside.

Home Life of Cancer

The home is very important to those typical of Cancer: after all it is thought that the crab carries its home on its back. It is where they retreat from the world, and they will try to create somewhere completely safe and secure where they can relax in peace, protected from the rigours of the world. Cancer also likes beautiful and valuable possessions, and fill their houses with art or collectibles, especially where these may accumulate in value. They may also have one area which is seen exclusively as their own, where they feel especially secure.

Gardens and gardening are also appreciated and enjoyed. They will usually be good at maintaining and decorating their homes, and will have plenty of food in the house: those typical of this sign like cooking and will enjoy entertaining and dinner parties. Many typical of Cancer like to lavish food and drink on any guests, and many also have pets, which will be loved and well looked after, or even spoiled.

Those typical of the sign of Cancer are usually very careful with their money and will like to have lots saved in the bank or hoarded under their bed. Those under this sign like to feel secure and material wealth does help – although it will never be enough in itself. It may appear to acquaintances, especially under the more extravagant signs, that Cancer is not paying their way or that they are being very cautious: this comes from a deep-seated fear and insecurity of having too little money. Cancer will always be generous, however, with their loved ones and family as they will want to extend their secure home and world to cover them too.

The typical parent influenced by Cancer will tend to be overly anxious about their offspring: in fact, they may spend their whole time worried and may try to curtail their child's freedom in an attempt to protect them from perceived danger: real or imagined. Despite the fact that they may be possessive of their youngster, they will do anything for them, and will nurture and care for them. They do like playing with youngsters, and will always remember birthdays, Christmas and any other important dates.

The typical Cancer child is very loving and wants affection, cuddles and hugs. Usually they are good natured and easy to look after and discipline. They can, however, become quite withdrawn if they feel hurt or threatened, and are very vulnerable to those who come over as being aggressive or domineering. This can become quite chronic, and if they have felt ignored, or even persecuted, as a child they may withdraw into their shell never to emerge, even in adult life.

Those influenced by this sign may appear quite moody, changing from happiness to quiet sadness because of an insult, rejection or misplaced word – or sometimes for no obvious reason at all. They may appear to be very emotional and weep and wail, although this crying can be quite manipulative, particularly if they have found this is a good means of getting their own way. If this does not work, they can also nip with those Cancer claws.

Many typical Cancer children also eat and drink a lot, especially when meals are especially appetising or if they derive some comfort from their consumption. If possible, they should be taught moderation or it may store up problems with overeating or alcohol or drug abuse in later life.

Those youngsters influenced by this sign may play for hours and hours by themselves and never get bored, or they may create invisible companions with whom they will speak and play. Painting, music, books and bright colours are of particular interest, and the Cancer youngster should be encouraged to develop their talents and learn to express themselves. Generally they have creative imaginations, and while these should be encouraged, sometimes they need to be shown the difference between the real world and fantasy, and sometimes even between truth and fiction.

Those children typical of Cancer will probably need lots of reassurance as they are easily hurt: the parent needs to coax them from their shell and then keep them there so that they can build self-assurance and trust. Those under Cancer can be very scared, even where their fears are quite vague, and they need to be taught that while some things may inspire anxiety, these can be managed once any threat is identified and minimised. If, however, they are coddled or overly protected, they may not be able face the real world with confidence. The parent must find a middle way between reassurance and protection, between protection and preparing them for the difficulties of the adult world.

A Cancer parent and Cancer child can respond very well together, having a mutual insight and understanding into the other. If either party feels threatened or insecure with the other, however, there may be great difficulties as they withdraw from each other or come out all claws blazing – or do both.

Work Life of Cancer

Those typical of Cancer are usually interested in security, and will be concerned with making sufficient money to feel secure. They can be very serious about work, and they will work seriously hard should that be required. They are reliable and disciplined, and will be prepared to take responsibility, either for their own area or in a management or educational role for others.

They can often see and understand the needs of others or of the business itself, and may nurture either or both as if it was a child. Being made to feel valued and appreciated is very important to the typical Cancer. Where this is not the case, or where those under this sign feel insulted or threatened, they may withdraw and say nothing – or they may become quite hostile and nippy. Cancer rarely forgets anything, which makes them an excellent worker, but they will also not forget any slight or perceived insult. To reward a Cancer for hard or good work is easy: they respond to money, bonuses or an increase in salary. Those under this sign will remember and appreciate other's hard work, and they will usually be fair and honest.

They can be very good at imparting knowledge or teaching, and they also prefer to have the most up-to-date equipment or tools.

Those influenced by Cancer like their workplace to be calm and secure and to feel appreciated and rewarded. Where this is the case, they will be excellent colleagues, working hard, being reliable and empathetic, and able and willing to take responsibility. If not, they may simply retreat from their work, doing the minimum necessary, and/or they may become resentful and crabby.

Famous People with the Sun Sign of Cancer

Louis Armstrong (musician), Yul Brynner (actor), Bill Cosby (comedian and actor), Tom Cruise (actor), Princess Diana (wife to Prince Charles), Harrison Ford (actor), Ernest Hemingway (writer), Henry VIII (monarch of England and serial wife murderer), Rembrandt (artist), Linda Ronstadt (singer), Jean-Paul Satre (writer and philosopher), Meryl Streep (actor).

Leo

NAME	The Lion
DATES	23 July-22 August
RULING PLANET	the Sun
ELEMENT	Fire
QUALITY	Fixed
COLOUR	yellow, orange
GEMSTONE	ruby, catseye, chryosolite
METAL	gold
ANIMAL	lion

Introduction and Background

Leo is the fifth sign of the zodiac, and is the Fixed Fire sign in the middle of the summer. As the Lion suggests, those under this sign have many characteristics believed to belong to that animal, such as pride, courage and even diffidence. Lions, however, can also be calculating and cruel when achieving what they want. As the Kings of the Jungle, they are also susceptible to flattery and insincere praise, but are at their happiest when they have a band of worshipping admirers. Leo, as mentioned above, is the Fixed Fire sign, and is associated with the high summer, which means those influenced by Leo often have a warm and sunny disposition. Fire brings about change and transformation, and Leo is one of the most creative of signs. Being a Fixed sign means that they can be loyal and open about themselves, but they can also be very stubborn and unmovable.

In love and friendship those typical of Leo make good partners and companions, and get on especially well with the other Fire signs Aries and Sagittarius, as well as the Air signs Gemini, Libra and Aquarius: the latter sign is the opposite sign to Leo and such matches can be the best or worst of relationships. Leo can be proud, vain and stubborn, but where there is enough honesty, passion and interest in the partner, those typical of this sign can be excellent and loyal lovers or friends. Where the partner can provide romance, warmth and admiration for the Leo, those under this sign will be warm and content within a long-term commitment; however, Leo enjoys being the centre of attention and may stray to anyone who shows sufficient interest.

The symbol for Leo is said to either be a depiction of the lion's tale or its mane.

Ruling Planet

The Ruling Planet of the sign of Leo is the Sun, the star of the solar system in which the Earth is located. Those under its influence expect everything to revolve or orbit around them. Things such as the self, essence, creativity and willpower are also associated with the Sun, along with characteristics such as warmth and pleasure.

Characteristics of Leo

These are obviously general and can be modified by many factors, not least the influence of the Ascendant Sign and the different planets in different Houses. Those typical of Leo who are frustrated or unhappy can exhibit some of the not-so-good characteristics, and of course a virtue in one situation can be a vice in another. Leo may have a deep sense of pride and dignity, which is usually considered to be a good thing. This is not, however, far from arrogance or contempt for others. Those influenced by this sign want to be on top, and being the best or first in their own area: the King of the Jungle. They may also need appreciation and recognition as the Leo can actually lack confidence and belief in themselves: after all, what is a king without loyal subjects to acknowledge their superiority? Leo is associated with the warmth and radiance of the sun, but those who spend too long a time in the sun can get badly burned.

Good Characteristics of Leo
- courageous and determined with much creative energy and drive
- can be excellent leaders and inspire others and get

the best from them
- have a warm and sunny disposition: little can dispel their optimism as long as the sun shines
- usually possess dignity, self-confidence and pride, as well as honesty and loyalty
- friendly, kind, hospitable and generous in nature
- have a tendency to be romantic, and are very interested in love and sex
- up-front and tend to take people for what they are, and also quick to forget insults or hurt
- may seem young or child-like
- need to be appreciated, recognised for what they are and complimented

Not So Good Characteristics of Leo
- stubborn and wilful, and can fall into a pattern or habit which they find it difficult to break
- drive to be in charge and on top: to be the king of the jungle; can lead their followers to ruin
- can become sulky and sullen if they feel they are not appreciated: especially unhappy when ignored or not noticed
- especially vain, a bit of a dandy, and can also take credit when not earned
- may have a tendency to be boastful and arrogant, as well as being gullible and can be easily swayed by flattery
- can be diffident, intolerant, self-righteous and uncaring, and even take pleasure in bringing others down

- on the outside all may appear to be well even when going through crises: find it hard to admit failure
- can appear to be diffident and lazy
- cold hearted when aggrieved and can be ruthless with enemies: a lion taking over a new pride will kill all the cubs

Appearance and Health of Leo

If someone has personality characteristics which are associated with Leo, they may also have the following physical traits:
- the face is oval
- noble and majestic in bearing
- can be tall or appear tall
- takes pride in appearance
- prominent hair or in males if bald this is also made a feature
- usually slim and athletic
- clear and loud voice

Those typical of Leo are usually healthy folk, but thrive when they feel loved. When they do not receive affection or believe they are unappreciated, those influenced by this sign can become unhappy about life, begin to complain a lot, and may look old and ill. Those typical of this sign need people to value them: the monarch needs subjects to venerate and assert them as rulers.

Fire signs do tend to be vulnerable to accidents, generally not taking enough care or getting themselves into dangerous situations, and Leo is no different. Illnesses which are associated with the sign tend to have a sudden onset such as fevers and acute illnesses. Leo feels it is necessary to recover quickly as they see any type of long-term or incapacitating illness as weakness, that they have let themselves, and any dependents, down by showing themselves to have human frailties. In the short-term, however, if bed-ridden they like a fuss to be made and to get as much attention as possible, which will help them get better.

Parts of the body which are associated with Leo are the heart, back and spine, including the circulation and blood supply, as well as sometimes the spleen, gonads, legs and ankles. That is not to say that these parts of the body may be especially susceptible to illness or particularly free from it. This strength or weakness can only be determined by doing a full birth chart.

Leo has great bursts of energy and stamina, and can be an inspiration, bringing warmth to all those around them. They do need to rest sometimes as they can run out of energy because of the great radiance they spend their time emitting. At this point they need to catnap, rest or relax – which can be mistaken for laziness – to recharge their batteries.

Likes and Dislikes of Leo

Likes of Leo
- sports and activity, either physical or mental exercise
- anything which gives pleasure

- creativity, dramatic events and theatre
- receiving presents, especially when much thought has been given to them and they have been personalised
- eating out in new or exotic restaurants
- being appreciated and complimented as long as it is sincere
- children and animals
- expensive and fashionable clothes and surroundings

Dislikes of Leo
- being hurt, especially physical pain
- doing little or nothing: any sedentary pastime
- being ignored or out of the limelight
- anything deceitful and untrue
- being laughed at or not being taken seriously
- making a fool of themselves
- being caught out or looking stupid

Love Life and Friendship of Leo

Those who are influenced by the zodiac sign of Leo will tend to be very attractive, energetic and outgoing, and will usually find it quite easy to attract a partner. Leo is romantic and passionate, as well as being open and honest. If a Leo is attracted to someone they will normally just come out and say it, and they expect the same honesty in return.

Although Leo can be quite insecure underneath it all, at least on the face of it they do see themselves as being superior, even if it is only in one aspect of life or love. They do like to be the dominant partner, and to be the stronger in the relationship. Although they like an attractive good-looking partner with some special skill or talent, they do not like to feel they are being outshone, or anyone that may eclipse them. Alternatively, they will not admire someone who is lacking talents – or at least who keeps their talents to themselves.

Those influenced by the sign are usually very openly romantic, and are extremely devoted and generous to the object of their affection, both emotionally and materially. Leo is at its happiest when they feel loved, and their partner can bask in their radiance. Being protective and supportive are both characteristics of Leo, and they will do anything for their loved ones: even if at great cost or sacrifice to themselves.

They will expect, however, to be adored and supported in return, and in some cases even worshipped and to be treated like royalty. They like to be king of their own castle. It is also important for those under this sign to feel appreciated, that they are very special and the envy of others – and they will want a partner who enhances their image and to make them proud. Total commitment and loyalty are required, and many influenced by Leo like their partner to be dependent on them in some way. They will generally, however, want a lot more than sex from a lasting relationship, and will expect their partner to be devoted to any children they may have.

Leo can be quite unrestrained and promiscuous and very much enjoy new experiences, although can be devastated when a partner is unfaithful. They can also be boastful: anyone wishing for a quiet fling should bear this in mind.

Often there will be a burst of sexual energy at the beginning of a new match, but sometimes the ardour for Leo can quickly subside, although they may want to continue the relationship as just friends. The physical side of a relationship may not be as important as the emotional.

Those influenced by this sign find failure intolerable, either sexually or in a relationship, and can be deeply hurt by either. If the Leo does have sexual problems they will rarely seek help. The jilted Leo can also take months to recover, and remains wary about new relationships for a long time afterwards.

Nevertheless, Leo can also be cold and cruel when they feel a relationship is over. Many find it difficult to make an end, especially if a partner has not actually done anything wrong, although some will simply be straightforward about their feelings. Where a partner is needy, and continues to be so even when the Leo is quite cool and distant, Leo can be cruel and take no regard of the partner's feelings, deliberately trying to wound. Being a proud creature, the typical Leo has disdain for those with no dignity. But they can find it difficult to break with a partner for whom they have regard but no love.

In friendship and love, Leo makes fine relationships

with the other Fire signs Aries and Sagittarius. They are also often attracted to the Air signs Gemini and Libra, as well as Aquarius, the Fixed Air sign of the zodiac, although these matches can be mixed: either complementary and beneficial, or confrontational and detrimental. Aquarius can help Leo to stop considering only themselves and allow others to shine. If the two signs can compromise and cooperate, this may produce a fine relationship. Leo may also be attracted to the intensity of Scorpio or the support of Cancer – but these matches may not last long.

Generally speaking, sunny Leo does not do well with Water and Earth signs as their wants and needs are usually not compatible. There can be brief and almost blazing attractions with any sign since Leo can be so attractive, and the more thoughtful signs may sometimes crave adventure. Often these are fleeting: Leo can be too hot to handle.

Friendships, however, can be long and enduring with Leo as long as friends realise that someone influenced by this sign hates to be outshone by anyone. This does not mean that those influenced by Leo do not like their friends and loved ones to be successful, only that they like to be more successful, at least in some area. Pride and dignity are intrinsic to Leo, and they can be very competitive, even with people to whom they are close – if they start to appear as rivals. Generally Leo make good friends as they are warm and sunny, even playful. They are also very generous, but they do like to appreciated in return. Leo may, however, find it difficult to have relaxed relationships with others of their own sign – although these friendships are rarely boring.

Leo just hates to be criticised or to be made a fool of, especially in public or in front of an audience. Anyone who is thought to have done this, no matter how close they may have been in the past, can be excluded and shunned. Similarly, if the Leo does not feel appreciated where they have helped or been especially generous, they may also drop a friend. Those with ambitions themselves or with special talents may find competition with Leo unrewarding and may choose not to be friends with those influenced by this sign.

Home Life of Leo

Those typical of the zodiacal sign of Leo will see their home as their own exclusive property, and will want to be acknowledged as masters within their house, even by loved ones: they like to be king of their castle. Leo is very territorial, and will need guests or loved ones to acknowledge their superiority. If this is the case, then they are very warm, generous and welcoming.

Leo will make a fine and tasteful place to live as they are very creative and love comfort. They are also practical around the house, and will mend or decorate as required. Those under this sign will also like to entertain, both to show off their home and to show how generous they can be to guests. Leo likes parties and will shower guests with food and drink. Visitors will also be welcome to stay for as long as they want. Leo will protect their homes and their loved ones with their lives, and will be good at dealing with domestic emergencies.

Those typical of the sign of Leo may not be very good with keeping control of their money and financial resources. Leo will always want to seem generous, extravagant and bounteous to their friends and family, and will never want to admit that they cannot afford to pay for something – or even anything. Similarly, they will want the best clothes, furniture and baubles for themselves as befits a king. Having the best of things is more important than having a healthy bank balance – unless of course the Leo sees their money as their source of power and regality, in which case they may actually be very careful and only appear to be especially generous.

Those influenced by this sign make excellent parents, and will be very diligent in raising and looking after their offspring. Leo is very warm and loving with youngsters, and will enjoy playing with and teaching children. They may be a little indulgent, especially when it comes to money or presents, although will try to instil honesty into their child. Leo very much wants to be proud of their youngsters, and they may make the child terrified of being a failure or not appearing to succeed. It is sometimes difficult to be brought up in the bright glare of the sunny Leo. Where a child is very able or athletic, the Leo parent can be so proud as to be boastful and arrogant.

The child which is typical of Leo is very warm and has a sunny disposition. They are usually very friendly with other children, especially where they are acknowledged as being in charge. They will be very generous and will be pleased if other youngsters play with their toys. Being the centre of attention is what pleases them most, and they will like their parents or playmates to treat them like royalty. Like with older Leo, youngsters love parties, especially if they are thrown for them, and being made a fuss of. Leo children do not like tidying their room or doing other chores around the house: these are simply too low for the high-born Leo.

Leo children usually have unlimited amounts of energy, and will tend to prefer physical games to ones which only use the intellect or imagination. Female Leo may be a tomboy. They are very adventurous and curious, even to the point of being reckless and endangering themselves: they should be closely supervised. They are also very friendly children, even with adults and strangers, and they need to be taught that some people can not be trusted and can even be dangerous – without making them afraid of everything. Despite their huge amount of stamina and energy, they will eventually get tired although after a brief but deep catnap they will usually be refreshed and soon playing and exploring again.

Leo youngsters need lots of love and affection, but they also need to learn discipline and to respect others as individuals and not just worshipful subjects. Leo can be boastful and arrogant, and should be shown that this is quite undignified: a truly confident or majestic person does not need to show off or boast. There is also a danger that they can be dictators within the home, and parents need to make sure that they do their fair share of jobs around the house: that sometimes even monarchs need to wash dishes. Leo is usually very generous with both their toys and their pocket money. They need to be taught restraint, and that money needs to be saved as well as spent.

Work Life of Leo

Leo loves to rule and hates to follow, and are excellent workers when they feel on top and where they are likely to get some reward from and recognition for their labours. Where the Leo is not in charge, they still need to feel that they are. Those typical of this sign are usually genuine and open, and they get on well with clients, customers and colleagues as they are generous with praise and compliments. When in turn they feel appreciated, Leo exhibits great self assurance, and they can be very good managers, inspiring loyalty and hard work from anyone working with them. Leo managers will usually be very considerate with their colleagues, and have great charm. Their workplace will look as opulent as possible, and will be comfortable and impressive. They are also very good in interviews, although the employer should be wary of exaggeration: a Leo will never underplay their talents and achievements.

Leo can be quite unforgiving of those who they feel are not working hard enough, or even worse those who make the Leo look stupid or undignified. They do find it difficult to admit defeat or that they may have made a mistake – and almost impossible to apologise if it has been their responsibility. They may also attempt to take the credit when things do go well, even if they have not been directly involved. They will enjoy and seek any job or business where they can shine and where they will be noticed.

Leo will work best in an environment where they can feel they are on top and where they will get recognition for their achievements. Those typical of this sign also do well where a sunny and optimistic personality is useful. They do less well in a rigid or regimented business, and where they have no control or credit for their work. They may also find it difficult to admit failure, and may be wholly unrealistic about their own abilities.

Famous People with the Sun Sign Leo

Lucille Ball (actress), Napoleon Bonaparte (general and emperor of France), Fidel Castro (revolutionary and head of Cuba), Bill Clinton (politician and former president of the USA), Alfred Hitchcock (film director), Mick Jagger (singer), Jacqui Kennedy-Onassis (wife of President John F. Kennedy), Madonna (singer and entertainer), Robert de Niro (actor), Robert Redford (actor), George Bernard Shaw (writer), Mae West (actress).

Virgo

NAME	The Virgin
DATES	23 August-22 September
RULING PLANET	Mercury
ELEMENT	Earth
QUALITY	Mutable
COLOUR	blue, yellowy green, brown
GEMSTONE	sapphire, opal, agate
METAL	mercury
ANIMAL	bat, porcupine, mink

Introduction and Background

Virgo is the sixth sign of the zodiac, and is the Mutable Earth sign. It is associated with practical adaptability to the many events and situations which can arise in the world or within life, and trying to improve both the world and themselves. Many things grow in earth and come to fruition, especially in the summer, and this sign is to do with change which results in a flowering: achieving the goal of improvement. Those influenced by Virgo strive for perfection through hard work, excellent communication and good organisation, even when the tasks are very mundane or ordinary. Virgo wishes to serve and to devote themselves to the welfare of people or the greater good. Those influenced by this sign can, however, worry that they are simply not good enough to complete any task as well as being anxious about other aspects of their lives. Health and growth cycles are also associated with Virgo.

In love and friendship, those typical of Virgo make good partners and companions, and get on especially well with the other Earth signs Taurus and Capricorn, as well as the Water signs Cancer, Scorpio and Pisces: the latter sign is the opposite sign to Virgo and such matches can be the best or worst of relationships. Virgo can be neat, demanding and overly practical, but where there is enough respect, trust and interest in the partner, those typical of this sign can be excellent and loyal lovers or friends. Where the partner can provide security, integrity and care for the Virgo those under this sign will be happy with a long-term, enduring commitment: those typical of Virgo will never want a one-night stand or brief affair.

The symbol for the zodiacal sign of Virgo is said to represent the Virgin. Virgins were often seen as being sacred. They were believed to have special insight and powers, such as healing, and knowledge about fertility and crops – even the ability to foresee and make prophecies. Often the deflowered virgin would lose her powers,. This deflowering, however, should be seen as a loss of spiritual purity rather than anything in the physical world. Virgo is an Earth sign and these signs are eminently practical and even earthy in outlook.

Ruling Planet

The Ruling Planet of Virgo is Mercury, first in the solar system, as well as being the smallest and nearest to the sun: Gemini is also ruled by this planet. Mercury was known to the Romans, and was the messenger of Jupiter and the gods (Hermes was his Greek counterpart). The planet is associated with communication, thought, intelligence and mental activities. Those with Virgo as a Sun Sign are more associated with the practical than Gemini, and in communicating such ideas widely. The metal mercury, which is known as quicksilver, is a heavy silvery liquid at room temperature.

Virgo is also associated with Vulcan, the Roman god of fire and metal-working, whose Greek counterpart was Hephaestus. Vulcan was skilled both with hands and mind. It was once thought that there was a planet Vulcan in an orbit between Mercury and the Sun.

Characteristics

These are obviously general and can be modified by many factors, not least the influence of the Ascendant Sign and the different planets in different Houses. Those typical of Virgo who are frustrated or unhappy can exhibit some of the not-so-good characteristics, and of course behaviour which is a benefit in some situations, such as passivity, modesty and hidden sexuality, may be bad in others. Virgo may exhibit prudish, repressed or eccentric behaviour if circumstances conspire against them. This may mask burning desire, almost completely hidden from everyone including themselves. Virgo desires to serve and to communicate, and can be painstaking and critical in their life and work. Sometimes this can lead to a dogmatic outlook on life which covers a deep lack of confidence.

Good Characteristics of Virgo
- hard working, well organised with a great attention to detail, yet also usually flexible in approach
- good communicator, logical and excellent at analysis and thoughtful examination
- altruistic, humane, helpful and sympathetic, especially for those in difficult circumstances
- responsible and dedicated, although often also subtle and adaptable
- modest, shy and has a tendency to be passive, although usually with a healthy attitude to sex
- neat and tidy, and may be associated with health, healing and hygiene
- deeply sensual and emotionally warm: their sexuality is often hidden and unexplored until the right partner is met
- charming, witty, good company and very communicative

Not So Good Characteristics of Virgo
- can be dogmatic and extremely critical of others, especially those considered lazy or undeserving
- has a tendency to be irritable, nervous, worried and somewhat cranky
- overly analytical about others and the self, and may be hypochondriacal, especially if extremely unhappy or frustrated
- undemonstrative, unsentimental and unresponsive
- prudish, obsessed with purity and in some circumstances repressed, either emotionally or sexually
- over demanding, both of themselves and others
- too perfectionist in outlook, although conversely may also be very untidy

Appearance and Health of Virgo

If someone has personality characteristics which are associated with Virgo, they may also have the following physical traits:
- upright in bearing and appears to have a straight body
- high forehead and high hair-line
- eyelids are often veiled, while the eyes are fine and soft
- generally fine featured: broad or pointed jaw and straight nose
- clean and tidy in appearance: often impeccably turned out
- hair almost always neat

Those typical of Virgo are usually healthy folk, although when worried or generally unhappy, this may translate into fears about their health and hypochondria. Many influenced by this sign have a huge range of medicine and remedies close at hand, and are interested in complementary and alternative forms of medicine.

Illnesses which are associated with Virgo can be conditions of the lymph system or the gastrointestinal tract, and especially the intestines, such as diarrhoea or constipation, appendicitis, diverticulitis, heart burn and indigestion. Virgo, however, is usually very good at looking after themselves and avoid many illnesses to which other Sun Signs may succumb. When sick, they do need sympathy and care to help them get better – even encouragement if they have become a bit melodramatic about their illness.

Parts of the body which are associated with Virgo are the intestines and colon, including the abdominal organs, spleen and duodenum, as well as sometimes the finger and toe nails. That is not to say that these parts of the body may be especially susceptible to illness or particularly free from it. This strength or weakness can only be determined by doing a full birth chart.

Virgo can be very adaptable, so avoiding or dealing with stress or other problems as they arise. Those influenced by this sign also, however, have a tendency to be nervous and restless, and it can be beneficial to have many practical things to keep them occupied.

These do have to be complex, intellectual or detailed enough to hold their interest.

Likes and Dislikes of Virgo

Likes of Virgo
- intellectual or complex challenges
- making lists of tasks
- detailed analysis or problems of challenges
- gardening and creative pursuits
- spirituality and even cults
- any activity which leads to self improvement
- helping others
- taking time for oneself, especially grooming, washing and choosing which clothes to wear
- small furry animals
- mimicking others

Dislikes of Virgo
- dirty, brash or noisy surroundings or people
- loud colours (or people)
- inactivity, although may only exercise to stay healthy
- crudeness, slovenliness and vulgarity
- disrupted plans and things being disorganised
- people who whinge or complain
- lies or deceit
- being held to any obligation
- admitting they have failed, made mistakes or have weaknesses

Love Life and Friendship of Virgo

Those influenced by the zodiacal sign of Virgo are not normally very romantic people in the hot-blooded sense, and they see relationships in quite practical terms. Most of those typical of Virgo want a long-term relationship, which once started they see as permanent and enduring. Many will be seeking the perfect match, someone suitable to marry and spend a lifetime with. Very few will ever desire a one-night stand or a brief fling, and Virgo can not become intimate with anyone who they do not trust. This sign is concerned with service and devotion, and when in love a Virgo will be devoted to their partner. If they can find their ideal partner, this will make both the Virgo and the partner extremely happy and fulfilled.

Those influenced by this sign may wait for a long time for the right person, and many are eminently practical about their choice of partner. They are looking for someone decent and respectable, somebody who is also clean and tidy, somebody to whom they can devote themselves and is worthy of their service. Virgo does not like unsubtle approaches or crude flirting: it is against their chaste and proper nature. They may well enjoy flirting in a platonic manner, and they will always do their best to never give their partner any cause to feel jealous. Indeed, once a Virgo has decided on a partner they will usually do their best to look after them through thick and thin. One problem may be that they actually do too much and leave nothing for their partner to contribute. They can often, however, correctly understand others and see what they need almost before they know it themselves. Virgo is not hugely hotly passionate, but they do love consistently and steadily, and are steadfast in their loyalty. It is unusual for Virgo to want to end a relationship.

Those typical of Virgo hate having their private lives discussed or to have anything intimate revealed. A partner should remember not to embarrass them in this way and to keep secrets completely. Those influenced by this sign can be very vulnerable to criticism, and will need attention and much affection when they are feeling low. As the sign which often seeks perfection, the last thing they want to feel is less than perfect themselves.

Generally Virgo enjoys sex and sees it as a normal healthy act. They do also cope well with celibacy, either in the short- or long-term, without too much difficulty. Those under this sign are often quite secure, but if they have had problems in the formative years, a few may have sexual problems. Those influenced by Virgo do need to feel safe and to trust their partner absolutely before becoming intimate. Virgo, however, is chaste and pure in mind yet not necessarily so in body: consummated love in the correct situation and environment will bring the Virgo true fulfilment.

As mentioned above, Virgo will rarely want to break off a relationship unless it is absolutely necessary. If, however, they feel their partner was not what they need, has changed in a negative way, has been unfaithful, is crude or course, or wants to pursue some course they see as indecent or unwholesome, Virgo will end a relationship. This will be done effectively, efficiently and without any turning back: once those influenced by this sign have made their mind up, little will change it, except perhaps if there are children involved. Virgo is essentially very practical and will do what is best for themselves and for any offspring. They will also put any failed partnership behind them, and then begin the search for the right person, learning from any mistakes. By searching, they believe that in the end they will make the perfect match.

In friendship and love, Virgo does well with the other Earth signs Taurus, Capricorn, and of course Virgo. They may also form good relationships with the Water signs Cancer, which can work very, and Scorpio, and especially Pisces, the Mutable Water sign. Pisces can show Virgo how to go with the flow and to develop new ideas, showing Virgo that perfection is neither possible nor desirable. When the two signs work together, this can be an excellent match; when not, things may be difficult or impossible.

Opposite and complementary signs can also work, and some influenced by this sign will do well with the Air sign Gemini and the Fire sign Sagittarius: the well-matched ephemeral and practical can benefit both. Generally speaking, however, Virgo will find the Air and Fire signs difficult and even stormy.

Friendships will be long and satisfying with Virgo as long as the friend is clean, decent and not extravagant, and has a wide range of interests which can stimulate those influenced by this sign. Virgo is extremely uncomfortable with outward shows of emotion, either positive or negative; and likes people who are calm and tranquil. They may not like to be cuddled or touched, except by those who are very close; and it can take quite a long time for a Virgo to even decide if they want to be someone's friend. Generally they have good taste, manners, and are very discriminating: which can make for an excellent companion, especially where there are shared areas of interest. Those influenced by this sign are extremely loyal to their friends, and will be gentle and considerate. Virgo is a good sign to have around when trouble strikes, as long as the situation can be controlled and bettered.

Indeed, Virgo is a sign which worries a lot and is very analytical. Friends who criticise should tread warily so as not to upset Virgo, although Virgo can be very critical – and very calculating in their criticism. They also find it very difficult to admit they were wrong about any topic or issue: such instances should be handled tactfully. Humour on the part of the friend may help should such issues need to be raised.

As Virgo does often suffer from nerves and anxiety themselves, someone close who has lots of problems – which they cannot or will not solve – can cause the Virgo to become a nervous wreck. Virgo tries to serve both friends and loved ones, and they feel unhappy or that they have failed when they cannot help.

Home Life of Virgo

Those typical of the zodiac sign of Virgo will make their home as domesticated as possible and see it as a base where they can look after family or loved ones or entertain visitors. Virgo loves their home to be neat, clean and tidy, and will prefer to be the one who does the cooking, cleaning, do-it-yourself and manages the mortgage and other household expenses. Although those under this sign like to serve, they also want to manage and will desire to be the head of the household and make all the decisions. Virgo believes they are much better at such things than other signs: that they are much the best when it comes to household chores and maintenance.

Many of those influenced by Virgo love to garden and grow things. They may take especial satisfaction in creating an orderly but beautiful garden with lots of flowering plants and culinary and medicinal herbs. They are rarely unoccupied, and while at home, if not looking after the house, finances or family, will probably be pursuing some leisure activity, hobby or interest, particularly where this improves their home, their family or themselves. Virgo will usually be most tranquil at home as it is the one place which they can control and organise above all others.

Virgo is generally very careful with money and wealth, and will be determined to get the best from their financial resources. They will always know exactly how much money they have on them, how much is available to them, and even how much their savings are worth in the bank. They will employ these resources effectively and efficiently, will never overextend themselves or get into debt unless it is really necessary, such as when there is an emergency – in fact they can make money sit up and squeak. Unlike the airy Libra, Virgo really is one sign that will always make sure the figures and the books balance.

As parent, Virgo will be devoted to their offspring, and will do anything for their family. They will encourage their child to be curious and questioning, and will help them with any practical pursuit and to acquire a good attention to detail. Those typical of this sign can worry excessively about their youngsters, especially about their health. In general they will not like their children to be dirty or untidy – not always possible or even desirable with active signs. They may also not like outward shows of affection or love, and may have problems acknowledging the depth of their emotions. Some children may find this slightly aloof and supremely practical nature a little difficult or unsatisfying.

Those children who are typical of Virgo spend much of their time trying to please a parent. They will rarely deliberately do anything they see as wrong, and will never knowingly question a parent's authority. Lying or deceiving is rarely a behaviour typical of Virgo. They may also be slow to develop their imaginative side. It should be remembered that it is as important to nurture the creative, as well as the practical, side of their nature.

They may quickly learn to do chores around the house, and help their mother or father with cleaning or tidying, even if they are only copying their actions. Generally, they are very inquisitive and learn very quickly, and will be among the first of their contemporaries to read and write. They will usually work hard and do well at school or hobbies, but may be a little perfectionist in outlook and not be sure when a project or activity is completed to a satisfactory level. Those youngsters influenced by Virgo may be very shy and retiring in company, and may be difficult at meal times as they can be quite fussy about what they eat, even when very young. They do not like to be teased, and may become very unhappy if people they do not know well are too familiar with them.

Virgo youngsters need a lot of compliments, physical contact and genuine admiration from their loved ones. There is a danger that they can feel worthless if they imagine they have failed in some way or not lived up to the high standards they set for themselves. It is particularly important for the young Virgo to feel they are physically attractive, or it may damage their relationships in later years as they can be quite awkward with the opposite sex. A misplaced word can shatter a Virgo's delicate ego, especially when it is about their appearance or cleanliness. The Virgo, however, can also set very high standards for their parents or siblings, and can be somewhat critical of every little failing in those with whom they live.

A Virgo parent and child will usually have a fine

relationship, although it is possible that they can both be a little too cool and critical of the other. As both are eminently practical, the Virgo parent should try to nurture the creative and imaginative side of their youngster.

Work Life of Virgo

In their work lives, Virgo is very hard working, thorough and reliable, and are very good at jobs or businesses where attention to detail is important. Generally they do not like to lead, but will be excellent where they have somebody to direct or manage them – and they can implement. They are very honest, polite and straightforward, while at the same time being methodical and good at analysis and solving complex problems. Those typical of Virgo are very fair and considering, and will always try to help people where possible. They offer stability and common sense in the work place. They prefer a business where it is not necessary 'to get your hands dirty', which is well organised and peaceful. Poor preparation will always irritate someone typical of this sign, and they will want the proper tools to complete the job.

Virgo can also be critical and demanding, especially where they feel someone is not pulling their weight or where a colleague is sloppy, ill-mannered or even slovenly. In this, they can be a bit judgmental and 'holier than thou'. Virgo also expects to be properly rewarded for the work that they complete: compliments simply will not suffice: the practical Virgo wants a material reward in the terms of a bonus or an increased salary. Being fair-minded themselves, they expect to be treated fairly and honestly.

Virgo will always do best in jobs where respectability, attention to detail, and where critical analysis is required. They do less well in any work where they have to lead or innovate, or where their is even a whiff of dishonesty. They will also do less well in a workplace which is dirty or badly organised.

Famous People with the Sun Sign Virgo

Lauren Bacall (actor), Anne Bancroft (actor), Leonard Bernstein (composer and conductor), Sean Connery (actor), Greta Garbo (actor), Michael Jackson (singer), Stephen King (writer), D. H. Lawrence (writer), Sophia Loren (actress), Peter Sellers (actor), Twiggy (model and actress).

Libra

NAME	The Scales
DATES	23 September-22 October
RULING PLANET	Venus
ELEMENT	Air
QUALITY	Cardinal
COLOUR	blue, green, purple, pink
GEMSTONE	emerald, opal
METAL	copper
ANIMAL	elephant

Introduction and Background

Libra is the seventh sign of the zodiac, is the Cardinal Air sign, and the first zodiac sign of the autumn, beginning at the equinox. The sign for Libra is the Scales, and this represents a need and striving for balance and harmony as a goal in all walks of life and work for those influenced by this sign. By trying to gain balance, by concentrating on one side of the scales, the Libra may only make their lives and themselves more unbalanced and lopsided. The scale turns on the fulcrum, and that point is the Libra. Those under this sign tend to be more interested in action, albeit it carefully considered. As the cardinal Air sign, Libra is concerned with ideas coming to fruition, although they make take a long time to flower – after being carefully weighed and measured. This Libra does actively, however, as the Cardinal Air sign. When a course of action has been properly considered, they will they do whatever is needed to pursue and complete it.

In love and friendship, those typical of Libra make good partners and companions, and get on especially well with the other Air signs Gemini and Aquarius, as well as the Fire signs Leo, Sagittarius and Aries: the latter sign is the opposite sign to Libra and such matches can be the best or worst of relationships. Libra can be calculating, overly idealistic and impractical, but where there is enough balance, thoughtfulness and interest in the partner, those typical of this sign can be excellent and loyal lovers or friends. Where the partner can provide harmony and energy, but still remain independent and undemanding, those under this sign will be happy with a long-term commitment as they are looking for their equal. However, they may take some time to find a suitable match, and may fall for an unsuitable partner.

The symbol for the zodiacal sign of Libra is the Scales, and Libra is the sign of justice, represented by the blindfolded Venus. Venus has the scales of Libra in one hand, and the sword of Mars (or Ares, the Greek god of war) in the other: Aries is the opposite sign of the zodiac to Libra. Libra starts at equinox of autumn, when the length of day equals the length of night,: night and day are balanced.

Ruling Planet

The Ruling Planet of the zodiac sign of Libra is Venus, second in the solar system, and often visible as a bright morning or evening star, when it can appear blue. It was known to the ancients, and Venus was the Roman god of love (Aphrodite was her Greek counterpart). Harmony, peace, beauty and art are associated with the planet, along with love and sensuality, of course. It is also associated with resources and possessions, and a comfortable home and life. Libra tends to show these characteristics in deeds rather than to keep them in their heads. Venus is the alchemical name for copper.

Characteristics of Libra

These are obviously general and can be modified by many factors, not least the influence of the Ascendant Sign and the different planets in different Houses. Those typical of Libra who are frustrated or unhappy may exhibit some of the not-so-good characteristics. Qualities such as being thoughtful and caring before taking any action, can in other circumstances be manipulative and calculating. The refined and sophisticated Libra may appear narcissistic and egotistical. Libra is frightened of being alone, as partnership and relationships are at the core of their being, although this is usually very well hidden.

Good Characteristics of Libra
- cooperative, communicative, good natured and a peacemaker or mediator in most situations
- will normally weigh matters carefully in the mind, but will then take decisive action where needed
- charming, sincere, trustworthy and good company
- romantic and loving, although often in a very practised, or even studied, way
- sophisticated, intelligent, artistic and refined
- interested in having fine and tranquil surroundings in which to live and work
- takes great care over appearance and usually has good taste and manners
- clear minded with an honourable outlook on the world
- strong beliefs and idealistic: will fight and even lead where there is a worthwhile cause

Not So Good Characteristics of Libra
- narcissistic, vain and egotistical, and has a tendency to be a bit of a fop or dandy
- can allow worries or fear to cause inaction, even when circumstances point to a positive direction
- has a tendency to consider too deeply resulting in being indecisive or inactive: this, and the above point, can lead those typical of this sign to be very

unhappy and frustrated as it goes against their nature
- actions may be manipulative, insincere and sly, simply to get what they want without ever coming out and asking for it
- may believe that their own refinement and intellect sets them above other mortals
- may be lazy and indolent and take little interest or care for those they see as inferior
- flirtatious, being interested in those of the opposite sex no matter what their age, and fickle in relationships
- can lose sight of themselves and forget they also have needs

Appearance and Health of Libra

If someone has personality characteristics which are associated with Libra, they may also have the following physical traits:
- rarely ugly and often good looking
- attractive and popular with the opposite sex
- the features of the face are fine
- the face is usually balanced
- charming smile and clear voice
- there is often a dimple, either in the cheeks, chin or knee
- graceful in movement
- athletic in build
- dresses well

Those influenced by Libra are usually healthy folk, although they do not cope well with being alone or being solitary, either in work or home life. They can also be crushed by the weight of responsibility carried on their shoulders, especially if there is nobody else there to shoulder the burden. This can result in illness, although they do tend to recover quickly as long as they are in calm, pleasant and tranquil surroundings with lots of care and attention: somewhere they can restore their equilibrium.

Libra often suffers from a variety of back conditions, as well as problems with the skin, kidneys and liver. Those influenced by this sign tend to put on a brave face when they are in pain or discomfort, and do get better much quicker if they are made a fuss of and pampered when recovering.

Parts of the body which are associated with Libra are the lower spine and the kidneys, including the adrenal glands and liver, as well as sometimes the skin including the external parts of the gonads. That is not to say that these parts of the body may be especially susceptible to illness or particularly free from it. This strength or weakness can only be determined by doing a full birth chart.

Libra needs to rest in a peaceful and harmonious environment, where they can relax and be themselves. They rarely rest when awake, however, as Libra spends most leisure time thinking and planning ahead. This can lead to those typical of this sign going round and round in circles. Often they need an activity which is absorbing enough to take their minds off their worries without being as equally stressful.

Likes and Dislikes of Libra

Likes of Libra
- pleasant and calm surroundings
- music and dancing
- having lots of friends and family around
- being admired and complimented
- being sent letters and presents such as cards and flowers
- conducting or taking part in a discussion where all the issues are set out in a logical way
- helping others
- fashionable and sophisticated clothes

Dislikes of Libra
- unpleasant or ugly environment or surroundings
- ill considered and loud or angry arguments
- having too little time to make up their minds
- being told what to do
- being lazy or sloppy in public
- being insulted or criticised, especially in reference to a loved one or cherished project

Love Life and Friendship of Libra

Those influenced by the zodiacal sign of Libra usually want a loving relationship above all else, but many are in love with the ideal of love itself, and not necessarily with their chosen partner. They do not see themselves as being whole until they have a partner with whom they can share their life and dreams – with whom they can achieve balance and harmony. Romance, then, is all, albeit in a quiet and relaxed manner, which will make the Libra glow and radiate. Libra has a deep-seated fear of being alone, and often do not make the best decision when choosing a partner, selecting someone who is unsuitable or will not meet their needs. They will then ignore, or at least be blind to, any failings which their partner may have, as their fear of loneliness is greater than being with the wrong person.

Libra likes to be courted but does not enjoy overly demonstrative behaviour; they are, in their turn, amusing, sophisticated, witty and charming. Quite quickly then can become emotionally dependent on their partner, and they expect to be cared for and to be supported through thick and thin. In return, however, Libra is relaxed and care-free in a relationship. Although they do expect faithfulness and loyalty, they do not want their partner to put too many emotional demands on them. They are prepared to overlook the odd little failing that their partner may have, or may not see it: putting their loved on a pedestal (where they like to be themselves).

Those influenced by this sign also want a partner who has separate interests and hobbies. Libra likes to be left alone to pursue their own projects or work with all the energy that they have. They also like to be admired, perhaps even put on a pedestal, and particularly like someone who can make them laugh. Libra is usually frugal and sensible with money, and excess or extravagance without the means of paying for it will anger or frustrate them.

Those influenced by this sign will normally enjoy a healthy and active sex life, but they may not be the most energetically sexual of signs. Libra looks for partnership, for a balance to the self, and if this can be found, will make an excellent match. If not, on the outside, they may seem calm and in control. They can be very influenced by what they absorb from the real world – television, the media and convention – into what they understand as attractiveness. Indeed, they may not be all confident in their sexuality or their appearance, comparing themselves to what they have seen in a fashion magazine or beauty show.

Libra tends to become more confident as they grow older, and often will have little assurance in themselves when young. At this point, they may want a partner in whose image they can mould themselves. As they become more mature, they will tend to seek a relationship of complementary equals. Provided, that is, that too much damage is not done along the way and they can feel more of a sense of self. A Libra who has not had this support may be very needy.

In general Libra will try to stay in a relationship where they feel they can get something out of it. They will attempt to win back a wavering partner using their great wit and charm as if they had only just met. If things do go wrong, the Libra will be very hurt, but will be determined to go back out into the world and find someone else. Those influenced by this sign are not able to cope very well when excess emotional demands are put on their shoulders: a partner would do well to remember this. It is one of the most likely reasons why a relationship with a Libra will end.

In friendship and love, those under the sign of Libra do well with the other Air signs Gemini and Aquarius as well as Libra. They can also do very well with the Fire signs Leo, where they can bask in that sign's warm glow, and Sagittarius, whose warm and adventurous nature can complement. The best (or worst) or partners is Aries, the Cardinal Fire sign. This match can just produce much fire and smoke, but particularly in the more mature, it can be an excellent relationship. Libra often has an underdeveloped sense of the self, whereas the Aries has, if anything, an overdeveloped ego. Aries can teach Libra how to have a separate identity, while Libra can teach Aries how to share with others. Generally, Libra does not do well with the Water and Earth signs.

Friendships can be lasting and special with those influenced by this sign. Generally those typical of Libra are warm, witty and entertaining companions, who like people and to be part of any social gathering. Libra is warm and open, and their sense of balance means that they will rarely do anything to upset or embarrass their friends. They will treat everyone they meet fairly and evenly. Indeed, they will do virtually anything for a friend in need, although too much emotional distress will quickly tire a Libra. Those influenced by this sign do become exhausted and will sometimes retreat from friends and loved ones so that they can rest and recuperate.

Libra can be very indecisive: their sense of self may be so ethereal that they just cannot make up their mind. If many decisions are to be made, the friend would do well to take as many as possible on themselves. Jealousy is something a Libra can feel if they believe those close to them are more attractive or talented than them. Those influenced by this sign can also swing up and down in their moods, from happiness and elation to dark depression. Attention and company will normally manage to lift a Libra's spirits, as can a compliment. Libra should not be left alone when they are depressed, or even when they are not. The thing a Libra hates the most is to feel alone or lonely.

Home Life of Libra

Those who are typical of the sign of Libra like to create a home where they can rest and recuperate in pleasant surroundings. They usually have very good taste, and will fill their homes with art and precious items which produce a feeling of harmony and balance. Similarly, they will enjoy soothing music on and decorate the house to match themselves. Libra does enjoy relaxing, listening to music, and just thinking and considering. They will normally keep their homes orderly and tidy, unless they are feeling aggrieved with someone else living in the house: either they are not pulling their weight or because the Libra does not feel appreciated. If the Libra swings this way, they may well do nothing at all around the house or may try to make it as messy as possible.

Those under this sign like to entertain and have people round to their homes as often as possible. They make very good hosts, and will be extremely charming, communicative and entertaining as well as providing plenty of excellent food and drink. Libra can be argumentative just for the sake of it, although they will not usually become heated: simply enjoying the the process and method of discussion. They can also be very indecisive and spend so much weighing every possibility that nothing around the house, such as repairs or decorating, ever gets done.

When it comes to money, wealth and the material world, those influenced by the sign of Libra will not be one of the signs who spend their time balancing their books. The Libra will see wealth and financial resources as a way of gaining something they want now, not in the future, usually something which gives them a feeling of peace or harmony. Money may somehow disappear into thin air as they spend it on purchases they believe they need or want – but then change their minds almost immediately. Those under this sign do not plan for the future.

The typical Libra parent can be relaxed and easy in bringing up their offspring. While this can teach the child to be independent and to think for themselves, it can also mean that the youngster is badly behaved and ill disciplined. Libra can spoil their children, and will give them plenty of affection and praise. Education is seen as being very important, and the Libra will spend a lot of time teaching and instructing their child. Generally, those typical of Libra are very proud of their children, especially if they are well groomed or especially sharp or bright.

The typical Libra child is usually very good looking, and will normally prefer to be well turned out and clean. They will be well behaved when they see the need for it. Even as youngsters they can be reasoned with – a sensible argument as to why the Libra youngster should do something will work well. Nevertheless, they are also very good at getting their own way, and in many cases can wrap adults around their little finger. Libra can argue black is white and white is black with equal conviction. As excellent and balanced arguers, it is sometimes difficult to disagree with them without looking foolish or petty. This can be a technique the child employs to get their own way, and there is a danger that they may end up being a bit spoiled and self-centred. This can be very difficult for the parent: badly behaved Libra children can be impossible as they will always find some way to justify what they have done – and may even end up persuading the parent that they have done nothing wrong.

Libra youngsters can be very indecisive and may always be in two minds about everything: they especially dislike being forced to make quick decisions without being given enough time to consider carefully. They are usually very sharp and bright, and often will be ahead of other children of a similar age. Libra youngsters do need helped to try to have their own opinions and express what they want: indeed, to make decisions which they would otherwise see as being too hasty or ill judged.

Like all children, young Libra needs measured attention and affection, but their privacy does need to be maintained.

A Libra parent with a Libra child will normally be fine, although two very indecisive people who can argue any case, combined in one home, may drive other signs mad.

Work Life of Libra

Those typical of Libra make very good workers, although they may not excel in businesses or jobs where they need to make quick decisions and then hastily act upon them. Libra likes to have time to weigh all courses of action and to discuss with as many other people as possible: in fact they see this thinking time as essential. As a consequence, though, they will rarely make stupid decisions.

Libra likes to work in a business where there are lots of people or colleagues, and will be particularly content when they are in a satisfying partnership. Those under this sign make and maintain many contacts, and will also have many ideas, sometimes quite extreme or revolutionary in nature. They will make many refinements to the benefit of the business.

Once they have decided something logically, they will believe it is the only sensible course of action. They can often lead, showing people what they believe is the right course of action, and taking their colleagues with them. The only problem is that where there decision is wrong, although this is rare, colleagues may find it impossible to persuade the Libra otherwise, and impossible to get any of their other work mates to do likewise.

Libra is very good at public relations, and will usually try to diffuse angry disagreements or disputes in the workplace, being very good mediators and able to see all points of view. They are always fair in their dealing with colleagues, and will never deliberately be unpleasant or disloyal to work mates. They are excellent counsellors and teachers. Those typical of this sign like work surroundings which are peaceful and harmonious, and they do not like work which causes arguments or friction.

Those typical of Libra make excellent workers where they have sufficient time to weigh up and consider all courses of action. They will communicate and liaise very well, and will always try to maintain harmonious relations between their work colleagues. They do less well when they feel pressurised into doing things before they are ready, and where a business is badly organised, poorly run, there are ongoing disputes, or where colleagues are bad tempered and unreasonable.

Famous People with the Sun Sign Libra

Julie Andrews (actor and singer), Brigitte Bardot
(actor), Jimmy Carter (politician and former president
of the USA), Dwight Eisenhower (politician and former
president of the USA), Mahatma Gandhi (politician and
pacifist leader of India), Bob Geldof (singer),
Jesse Jackson (politician), Deborah Kerr (actor),
John Lennon (singer), Franz Liszt (composer),
George Peppard (actor), Oscar Wilde (writer and wit).

Scorpio ♏

NAME	The Scorpion (Scorpious)
DATES	21 October-21 November
RULING PLANET	Mars and Pluto
ELEMENT	Water
QUALITY	Fixed
COLOUR	deep red, bluey green, black
GEMSTONE	turquoise, snakestone, ruby, topaz
METAL	iron, steel
ANIMAL	wolf, scorpion

Introduction and Background

Scorpio is the eighth sign of the zodiac, and is the Fixed Water sign. Still waters run deep, and as the Fixed sign so do those typical of this sign, so deep as to be virtually impenetrable: there is so much hidden beneath the surface. Scorpio may not be comprehended by others, but they have great insight into others themselves, and will usually understand their drives and motives. As the the Scorpion suggests, Scorpio can also be very dangerous to know with the deadly sting in the tail: those influenced by this sign can sometimes be vindictive and even sadistic. Scorpions are also one of the toughest of creatures, and survive in many harsh and difficult environments. Scorpio falls in autumn and covers the period of Halloween, and magic and transformation, as well as the cycle of life and death, are associated with this sign.

In love and friendship, those typical of Scorpio make good partners and companions, and get on especially well with the other Water signs Cancer and Pisces, as well as the Earth signs Virgo, Capricorn and Taurus: the latter sign is the opposite sign to Scorpio and such matches can be the best or worst of relationships. Scorpio can be intense, uncommunicative and domineering, but where there is enough depth, sensuality and interest in the partner, those typical of this sign can be excellent and loyal lovers or friends. Where the partner can provide physical love, solidity and passion for the Scorpio, those under this sign will be happy with a long-term, enduring commitment. Those typical of Scorpio are very physical and when unsatisfied within a relationship will go elsewhere.

Scorpio is a large constellation, which lies between Libra and Sagittarius, and is crossed by the milky way. It contains a very bright star, and the name is from the Latin for scorpion. The symbol for the zodiacal sign is a depiction either of the sting in the scorpion's tale or, it has also been suggested, the male genitals. Scorpio is also associated with the phoenix, the mythical bird which could rise from its own ashes.

Ruling Planets

The zodiac sign of Scorpio has two Ruling Planets: Mars and Pluto.

Mars, also known as the Red Planet, is the fourth in the solar system. It was known to the ancients, and Mars was the Roman god of war (Ares was his Greek counterpart), who was the father of Romulus and Remus. Those associated with the planet may have much physical energy, and be bold and courageous. It is also associated with action, anger and desires. Mars, however, was hero to the underdog and an inspiration in battles of all kinds. Mars is the alchemical name for iron.

Pluto is the ninth planet in the solar system, and is furthest from the sun. It was only discovered in 1930, although it had been proposed for some time before that. Pluto is associated in astrology with death, destruction, rebirth, regeneration and transformation, as well as power. In Greek mythology, Pluto was the god of the underworld. His Roman counterpart was Hades.

Characteristics of Scorpio

These are obviously general and can be modified by many factors, not least the influence of the Ascendant

Sign and the different planets in different Houses. Those typical of Scorpio who are frustrated or unhappy can exhibit some of the not-so-good characteristics. Traits which can be seen as virtues, such as caring passionately or being self-critical, can in another light be seen as vices, such as being jealous or self-destructive. Scorpio does not like to reveal the true self, but when they have some goal or objective, good or bad, it is virtually impossible to stop them from attaining it. They are often very good at reading others, and may have a penetrating insight into motive.

Good Characteristics of Scorpio
- can have a deep insight and can comprehend failings, being difficult to shock
- long memory
- probing, piercing, incisive and investigative, with the self, other people or the world
- deep concern and compassion for others even when their situations may be of their own doing
- sensual, passionate and deeply emotional
- magnetic personality and dynamic: Scorpio is usually very attractive people when they want to be
- has the ability to concentrate single-mindedly on one task and achieve it, no matter what the cost or odds against doing so
- protective and loyal: will do anything for a friend or family member in need
- tenacious and determined, no matter what obstacles lie in the way of their goal

Not So Good Characteristics of Scorpio
- suspicious of the motives of others and intolerant of anything seen as bad or undesirable
- secretive and difficult to get to know as the real Scorpio remains hidden even to family and close one
- long memory and vengeful: remembers every perceived insult (or, it should be said, insincere compliment)
- jealous and possessive of anything seen as a belonging: people or items
- has a tendency to be cunning and sly in their dealings with others, using their own weaknesses or foibles to the Scorpio's advantage
- moody
- self-destructive, frightening, cruel and dangerous: sadistic or masochistic
- quick tempered and maybe quite insulting: there is always the sting in the tail
- stubborn, zealous and obstinate: will pursue a course of action or inaction even when it has been shown to be wrong

Appearance and Health of Scorpio

If someone has personality characteristics which are associated with Scorpio, they may also have the following physical traits:
- piercing eyes and thick eyebrows
- strong and athletic in build but not usually very tall
- strong features but usually attractive

- has a tendency to be slender but with broad shoulders
- often have a broad face and wide forehead
- thick neck
- males often have hairy arms and legs
- may incline head downwards when regarding somebody

Those typical of Scorpio are usually healthy folk, but when they do become ill it can often be very serious or even life threatening. Usually they will have the determination to get better, but if they do too much, either work, sport or in any aspect of life or if they get depressed, they may damage their own health, or even actively seek to do so. However, even when very ill, Scorpio can have the ability to recover completely.

Scorpio can also be accident prone, and other conditions associated with this sign are nose and throat conditions as well as hernias, piles, bladder diseases and problems with the reproductive organs.

Parts of the body which are associated with Scorpio are the gonads, reproductive tract and urinary tract, as well as sometimes the nose, throat, back and legs. That is not to say that these parts of the body may be especially susceptible to illness or particularly free from it. This strength or weakness can only be determined by doing a full birth chart.

Those under this sign find it very difficult to relax, and may actually not want to. This can make leisure time very difficult, and especially holidays or time away from work. Scorpio may prefer to continue to work or exercise, even when damaging to health and when they need rest and recuperation. If taking time off, it is often beneficial to have some activity or hobby to fill the gap between work or training. Often mental challenges can be beneficial, especially when combined with elements which are physical but not too taxing.

Likes and Dislikes of Scorpio

Likes of Scorpio

- any activity which occupies the mind or body, but particularly where tactics are required
- secrets and mysteries
- winning: Scorpio can be very competitive: physically or mentally
- sex
- being complimented and recognised for what they have done as long as it merits it
- their homes

Dislikes of Scorpio

- being quizzed about themselves or being analysed
- being insincerely flattered or getting too many compliments when not warranted
- trusting strangers

Love Life and Friendship of Scorpio

Those who are influenced by the zodiacal sign of Scorpio are intense and constant in their relationships.

This love or desire is usually focused on one person only, and their attachment is long and enduring. This main relationship is vitally important to Scorpio, and they will live their life and achieve their ambitions either through or with their partner. They will also support and encourage a partner to shine, and will never be put off by their partner achieving more than them. The success of the Scorpio is the success of the relationship.

Those under this sign can be very dependent on their partner, but this is kept hidden and secret. Yet at the same time they will see themselves as the dominant one who is in control. Often this dominance will also be hidden, as Scorpio is very shrewd, and may see letting their partner think that they are in control is the best way of actually getting their own way.

Generally Scorpio does not have any trouble attracting partners, and the object of their affections will in turn be strongly attracted to those influenced by this sign. Scorpio can be either subtle or forward depending on which approach they believe will succeed with their object of their affection. One of the main characteristics of the sign is that, while they may see and understand other people, they can rarely be seen or understood themselves if they do not wish to be. Those influenced by this sign may also take some considerable time to finally settle on a partner they desire, but once they have decided they are completely committed.

Once a suitable partner has been found, Scorpio

will make them their whole life, and will have a deep and abiding love. This love can be quite possessive and domineering, and in turn those influenced by this sign rely more and more on their partner. Scorpio is not demonstrative in public, only when they feel they are out of the sight of others will they be tender, intimate and close with their loved one. They are not as a rule especially romantic: the romance of the relationship is being with their partner. Those influenced by Scorpio are always true to their own feelings, but partners should remember that they revel in the time spent alone with their partner, especially when they can share some secret or confidence. However, they are always wary of compliments and praise, usually if they realise this is insincere or just flattery to manipulate the Scorpio. Those influenced by this sign are rarely duped.

Typical Scorpio is very interested in sex, probably the most interested of the signs of the zodiac, and it is very important to their whole being. They use sex as a release from the frustration and hidden passion which lies beneath the surface: normally not apparent to those who do not know them well. Scorpio can lead exciting sex lives, and many are willing to experiment, while others are just glad to be intimate with their chosen partner. It should be said that while a Scorpio will usually be faithful when within a relationship, if the physical side has ceased or become unsatisfactory, they will go outside their main relationship to find a sexual partner.

Those typical of Scorpio are usually the strong partner in a relationship, and as such if they wish to finish it they will just go ahead and do so. This is most often the case when the relationship has deteriorated and cannot be retrieved, sometimes exacerbated or caused when the physical side diminishes. When this happens, as mentioned above, the Scorpio will find a new partner if they so wish. If, however, it is Scorpio's partner who breaks up the relationship, then those influenced by this sign can be very angry, vengeful and vindictive. They will want revenge, and will bear a hurt and a grudge for as much time as it takes from them to feel that they have got even. Scorpio can be blatant in retribution, but they can also be subtle and devious, enjoying their revenge as it unfolds over a considerable time. Those under this sign may eventually forgive, but they never forget. And scorpions have a venomous sting.

In friendship and love, those influenced by the sign of Scorpio do well with the other Water signs Cancer and Pisces. They can also form satisfying relationships or friendships with the Earth signs Virgo and Capricorn, and especially with Taurus. Where this works, it can produce a match made in heaven; where not, it can come straight from hell. Taurus is very solid and down to earth, as well as being concerned with pleasure and appreciation. Scorpio can learn to stop being so critical and calculating, and to enjoy the sensual pleasures of life along with the steady and calm bull.

Generally Scorpio does not do well with the Fire and Air signs, and relationships with Aries, Gemini, Leo and Aquarius can all be difficult and unrewarding. Sometimes, however, opposites do attract and complement, and Scorpio shares the Ruling Planet Mars along with Aries.

Friendships can be long and fulfilling with Scorpio, as long as the friend appreciates the Scorpio for their talents. Those influenced by this sign do not like to be praised or complimented without very good reason. They are also very intuitive, and once they get to know somebody, will usually also learn their secrets or guess when they are hiding something. Scorpio is an excellent judge of character, and some may find this very off putting: some like to retain an air of mystery, but those influenced by this sign may work things out or just know. Scorpio does not usually have very many friends, in fact does not really much like company, but the friendships which are maintained are close and enduring. The Scorpio will do most anything for these friends, and also give good advice and help when needed. They do not gossip, and as they harbour so many secrets of their own, they are also excellent at keeping other people's.

Home Life of Scorpio

Those typical of the sign of Scorpio see their home as very much their own territory and a place they will want to control. They create a self-contained house where they are the masters, if they can: they may find it much harder to control or manipulate their children. Scorpio will prefer an orderly, comfortable and tasteful home, which will be kept clean. They may also have a room or area which they see as their own, where they can retreat to think and consider, which they do not want to share with other people. Those influenced by this sign often need to spend quite a lot of time alone, either in the home or off on some solitary pursuit or leisure activity. During these times of contemplation, they do not like being disturbed, and may get quite angry should anyone do so. Generally, Scorpio does not like their home being invaded, even sometimes by guests, and will protect it and their loved ones with great determination and even aggression. Often they will put up with visitors only with great sufferance.

When it comes to money, those influenced by this sign are very much of the mind that neither a lender nor a borrower be. They tend to be careful with money, and are rarely ever wasteful. Scorpio likes to plan and scheme, and their attitude to their wealth is no different. Scorpio will usually have plenty of financial resources, although their money may be hidden away in a bank account outwith the knowledge of even close friends and family. That is not to say that Scorpio will not use money. They will employ it when it is needed or where they have some goal or ambition: money being the means to an end rather than the end itself.

The typical Scorpio parent can be a very strict disciplinarian, especially concerning rules which they have set and maintain themselves. They will want to keep their offspring occupied with all sorts of activities, usually outdoor if possible. They do set youngsters very high standards, which are sometimes very hard to meet and may leave the child feeling as if they have failed. Those under Scorpio, as a Fixed sign, can be a bit set in their ways, and find it difficult to adjust to the values and outlooks of young people, and especially teenagers. This can be an area of conflict. They will, however, do their utmost to remain on good terms with their offspring as they grow up. One thing is certainly constant: the Scorpio parent cares passionately about their children and will do anything for them, even if it means protecting them with their life.

The typical Scorpio child is quick to learn and has a questing mind, usually picking things up without any trouble. Often it may seem as if they can understand adults' problems or discussions easily, even when they are quite young. Youngsters typical of this sign are usually very focused and certain of their own minds, and will be good, and sometimes even ruthless, at getting what they want. While they will be very loving children, and will always be loyal and caring to those to whom they are close, they can also exact revenge on anyone outwith their immediate loved ones who slights them, takes a possession or toy without asking, or damages or misuses a Scorpio's belongings. Scorpio youngsters may get into quite a few scrapes, both physical and mental, and will always fight or argue to win. They are stoic about their own pain, both physical and mental, yet may be quite content to cause pain in others.

Scorpio children look to a stronger or wiser person for knowledge and instruction, and will not listen to someone they believe is inferior. They are good at finding out the secrets of others, both intuitively and by excellent reasoning, but Scorpio youngsters will rarely reveal much of their own emotions or feelings. Indeed the more 'secret' an area, the more fascinated the Scorpio child will be in trying to discover it. They can be a little dark compared to other signs. They are also almost always suspicious of people they do not know or have only met for the first time.

It is important that they are taught to respect others, and not to react violently, either physically or emotionally, when they are wounded. Scorpio, both children and adults, can lash out if hurt, or may enjoy their revenge in a slower but more considered way. Either way, if possible they should be taught to forgive those who may anger them rather than seek retribution.

Those typical of Scorpio need their own 'hidden' and secure place, away from others, where they can think and consider.

A Scorpio child with a Scorpio parent may be a very intense occurrence, as both parties can comprehend the other and intuitively know what they are thinking. Much friction can arise, although mutual loyalty will normally pull through.

Work Life of Scorpio

Those typical of Scorpio are excellent workers, especially in areas where they can lead, where there are difficult projects to see through to completion, or where there is a need for their penetrating analytical skills. They are very tenacious and determined, and will usually overcome any obstacle to meet their objective. If this means treading on toes or bulldozing their way through, they will do it. Most of their colleagues will follow, however, as Scorpio is very good at understanding people and understanding what drives them. Indeed, they will quite quickly know peoples' secrets and be able to sense how they are reacting to any situation. Scorpio expects loyalty, but in return will do anything for colleagues they trust and who need their help, either at work or in their personal lives.

Scorpio can be highly motivated, ambitious and somewhat ruthless, but this may never become apparent to their colleagues. If they want to make the business successful all to the good, but if their real motivation is personal gain they may simply please themselves. Also, where the business is seen as an enemy, the Scorpio may do their damnedest to see that it fails. This is unusual as they are usually too loyal. The same drives that can overcome virtually any problem, can be turned against an individual or their work – and the focus for the Scorpio may never become apparent.

Scorpio does very well where they can lead,

overcome problems, feel committed to the business or enterprise, or where a deeply analytical approach is needed. They do less well where they must do what others want without question, where they are overly managed and analysed themselves, or where they actively do not like an enterprise or their colleagues.

Famous People with the Sun Sign Scorpio

Prince Charles (heir to the British throne),
Hillary Clinton (politician and wife of the former
president of the USA), Marie Curie (scientist),
Indira Gandhi (politician and former leader of India),
Bill Gates (businessman and founder of Microsoft),
Billy Graham (US religious leader),
Goldie Hawn (actor), Pablo Picasso (artist),
Winona Ryder (actor), Dylan Thomas (poet).

Sagittarius

NAME	The Archer
DATES	22 November-21 December
RULING PLANET	Jupiter
ELEMENT	Fire
QUALITY	Mutable
COLOUR	blue, purple, white
GEMSTONE	jacinth, lapis lazuli, turquoise
METAL	tin
ANIMAL	horse, dog

Introduction and Background

Sagittarius is the ninth sign of the zodiac, and is the Mutable Fire sign. It is also the last sign of the autumn, and heralds the coming of full winter. As the Mutable Fire sign, Sagittarius is very adaptable to virtually any situation, and seek to explore and travel in work, relationships and life. The archer aims at the target, and often hits the mark. When they have brought down their prey or indeed it escapes, Sagittarius then moves on to another quarry. Those influenced by this sign crave freedom beyond anything, and when placed in a restricted or narrow environment they can become very unhappy and frustrated. Those typical of Sagittarius are usually very warm and optimistic, and have the ability to change negative situations for the better. They tend to see the best in most events and people, even when others might see little good.

In love and friendship, those typical of Sagittarius make good partners and companions, and get on especially well with the other Fire signs Aries and Leo, as well as the Air signs Libra, Aquarius and Gemini: the latter sign is the opposite sign to Sagittarius and such matches can be the best or worst of relationships. Sagittarius can be flighty, unwilling to commit, and has a tendency to become easily bored, but where there is enough balance, adaptability and interest in the partner, those typical of this sign can be excellent and loyal lovers or friends. Where the partner can provide excitement and stimulation but let those typical of this sign remain independent and free, those under this sign will be happy with a long-term commitment. However, commitment may be difficult for Sagittarius as they can feel trapped, and they may be content with a string of short-term flings.

Sagittarius a large and noticeable constellation in the southern hemisphere, which lies between Scorpio and Capricorn. It is crossed by the milky way. The name is from the Latin for archer, and the symbol for Sagittarius is an arrow, representing the Archer.

Sagittarius is associated with Diana, the huntress from Greek Mythology, who is also known as Artemis – as well as the Centaur, which was half human and half horse.

Ruling Planet

The Ruling Planet for the zodiac sign of Sagittarius is Jupiter. Jupiter is the largest of the planets in the solar system, and the fifth from the Sun. In Roman mythology, Jupiter was the king and ruler of the Olympian gods, and his Greek counterpart was Zeus. In astrology Jupiter is associated with wisdom and intelligence, as well as exploration, abundance and growth. The god was also pictured as being fun-loving and jovial, indulging life to the full. Beliefs, personal philosophy and education are also connected to this planet.

Characteristics of Sagittarius

These are obviously general and can be modified by many factors, not least the influence of the Ascendant Sign and the different planets in different Houses. Those typical of Sagittarius who are frustrated or unhappy can exhibit some of the not so good characteristics. Positive aspects of those influenced by this sign, such as a happy-go-lucky attitude to life and boundless enthusiasm and inspiration, can in other circumstances be quite negative. Someone who is happy-go-lucky may not plan when the situation warrants it, and boundless enthusiasm joined with inspiration may lead the Sagittarius to be a preachy fanatic, either spiritually or in their life or work. Sagittarius hates to feel bound or walled in, and dislike rules and order, possessive friends or partners, and anyone who is stuck in their ways or narrow minded. They themselves, however, may be quite dogmatic.

Good Characteristics of Sagittarius
- very open, fair-minded, free thinking and honest with people
- warm, abundant and generous with a happy and fun-loving nature
- confident and optimistic: has a tendency to see the best in people and events, even if they appear negative to others
- idealistic and just
- happy-go-lucky: will trust to chance
- spiritual and sensual
- endless enthusiasm for projects which hold interest
- can be quite inspiring and stimulating for all those around them
- rarely holds grudges, even with extreme provocation, and forgives quickly

Not So Good Characteristics of Sagittarius
- argumentative and somewhat hot-headed: often cannot leave an angry discussion no matter how far it degenerates
- inability to acknowledge sad or negative feelings, may even hide them no matter how much it hurts

- can be forgetful, blundering and inept
- lack of foresight and planning: leaves too much to chance
- may be a bit of a gambler at heart: trusting to luck
- preachy, dogmatic and can be tactless as they can believe that they know best
- can be angry with those who will not acknowledge their skills or talents, especially if integrity is questioned
- will not commit and has a deep-seated fear of losing freedom in relationships or any aspect of life
- can be indulgent, with food, drink or any of the good things in life

Appearance and Health of Sagittarius

If someone has personality characteristics which are associated with Sagittarius, then they may also have the following physical traits:

- active, constantly on the move, and physically strong
- eyes which sparkle with humour
- handsome or fine featured: usually very smiley, reflecting an optimistic outlook on life
- uses many hands, arms and gestures when speaking, especially when connected with a topic which is of interesting to them
- may have a tendency to be overweight

Those typical of Sagittarius are usually healthy folk, and will normally overcome adversity or poor health.

Routine and the mundane sap Sagittarius's energy, and if confined to bed they will become extremely frustrated and unhappy.

Fire signs are susceptible to accidents, and those influenced by Sagittarius take unnecessary risks and too little care. They can often injure themselves by walking into things, tripping and falling; or from dangerous pursuits or extreme sports. Conditions connected with those associated with this sign are often arthritic or rheumatic, as well as diseases of the hips and legs. There may also be problems from overindulgence, leading to being overweight or even obese.

Parts of the body which are associated with Sagittarius are the liver, hips, and thighs, including the pelvis and femurs, as well as sometimes the nerves and circulation in this area. That is not to say that these parts of the body may be especially susceptible to illness or particularly free from it. This strength or weakness can only be determined by doing a full birth chart.

Sagittarius can find it difficult and often unnecessary to rest. Most tiring is to be bored or to be in a suffocating relationship or constricting job. Not that they do not like their beds or to sleep, as then they can think or dream without distraction.

Likes and Dislikes of Sagittarius

Likes of Sagittarius
- being free to make choices as desired

- anything alternative or against orthodoxy
- travelling, exploring and being on the move
- food and drink: all the good things of life
- entertaining, parties and having fun
- taking risks, either in leisure pursuits or by gambling money
- solving problems, as long as this does not take too long
- belief system and spirituality

Dislikes of Sagittarius
- others being critical or disapproving
- promises being coerced or made, especially when these might curtail freedom
- bureaucracy, rules or laws which seem unnecessary
- paperwork and form filling
- tight clothes
- integrity being questioned

Love Life and Friendship of Sagittarius

Those influenced by the zodiacal sign of Sagittarius find love, relationships and sex to be part of the adventure of their lives. To some this will simply be meeting new people in interesting places, while to others the adventure may be in one relationship and with one partner. For the relationship to continue beyond the short-term, those influenced by this sign must meet someone who is their equal, both intellectually, sexually and emotionally, someone who they find stimulating and even exciting. Sagittarius hates to be bored and hates to be tied down, but a relationship which is liberating will be quite fulfilling. Where it is constricting or the partner is inferior, the Sagittarius will soon pack up and gallop off into the sunset. The world is a fascinating place, and they will find someone more suitable. Partners should be enthusiastic and spontaneous.

Sagittarius is both warm and charming. If they find someone interesting, they will pursue them with determination, but often also with guile and subtlety. As the hunter of the zodiac, those influenced by this sign may use strategy to capture their quarry. Alternatively, they will simply be open and straightforward: they will use which ever approach gives them the greater chance of success. This may mean that they can be a bit reckless at times, certainly they are never coy: some may find the chase more exciting than the capture, and some may hunt unsuitable or even dangerous game. Sagittarius loves to travel and explore, and are particularly fond of the holiday romance. They are not interested in detail and complications, and by the time they have returned to wherever they call their home they will usually have moved on.

For a long-term relationship, those typical of Sagittarius need someone who they see as an equal, someone who will explore the wonders of the world with them, or at least encourage them to do so. They like to be entertained and amused by their loved one. Those influenced by this sign are friendly and outgoing, and will find many people of interest. Those who are partners to a Sagittarius should be very careful not to show any jealousy, as those influenced by this sign hate their loved ones to be possessive or to feel that their freedom has been curtailed. Also those who want a quiet ordered life without change or excitement should not seek Sagittarius as long-term partner, although it may be great fun.

Sagittarius more than anything loath to feel trapped, and they may not be the kind of people who want to settle down in a traditional or conservative way. They detest being told what to do: hinting and encouraging will always be a better approach. They also expect complete honesty, and will be total honest with their partner: as long as this happens they will feel secure. Those influenced by Sagittarius are generally very content anyway, but when they feel loved and appreciated they glow with happiness. They also very much enjoy physical contact, and like to be hugged and cuddled.

Sagittarius loves life, adventure, sex and pleasure, and also enjoy any physical contact. They can be a bit careless in who they choose as a partner: sometimes the adventure and hunt of the relationship is more important than who exactly the partner is – this can get them into trouble. As mentioned above, however, a good sex life will never be enough for a Sagittarian: they need someone who is their intellectual equal. Those influenced by this sign can be somewhat flighty, and even in an established or (too) stable relationship can stray. Probably more than any other sign, those typical of Sagittarius may have an affair, usually short lived, burning itself out once the novelty has passed.

Sagittarius will stay with a partner and remain faithful as long as their attention is kept and as long as they feel stimulated. If bored or discontent, they will move on, as they will if their partner is prone to being jealous. A jealous partner will always find something to concern them with Sagittarius: they are too interested in others to ever be satisfied with only one exclusive relationship.

In love or friendship, Sagittarius does well with the other Fire signs Aries and Leo, as well as Sagittarius. They also can form good matches with the Air signs Libra and Aquarius, and also with Gemini, their opposite sign and the Cardinal Air sign. Where they two can complement and encourage each other, this can be an excellent match. There may, however, be too little substance in such a friendship or relationship, and it may never get going or burn itself out. Sagittarius can take too little time to think and may lack the depth for insight. Gemini can provide this, and in return can benefit from the single-mindedness and the focus of Sagittarius. Generally Sagittarius does not do well with the Water and Earth signs: generally freedom and adventure is not what those signs desire. Taurus, Scorpio and Virgo will usually be the worst of relationships, but in some cases the depth or solidity of these signs may complement.

Sagittarians can be excellent friends, and these

relationships can be long-term, although generally those influenced by this sign prefer to have many more casual friendships than one or two very close ones. Those typical of Sagittarius are not judgmental and will be friends with anyone of any age, background, ethnicity or sexual orientation as long as the potential friend is not narrow-minded, is interesting, and comes up to Sagittarius's standards. Those influenced by this sign can say exactly what they think, even if they are being quite critical, and some friends may find this off putting or irritating. Being straightforward and up front is not everyone's idea of friendship: Sagittarius is not always the most subtle of signs when it comes to saying what they think.

If they feel insulted or that they are being taken advantage of, like all the Fire signs, they can be quite aggressive and even violent. More usually it will be the barbed and wounding words that the Sagittarian uses rather than their fists. However, those influenced by this sign will quickly forget and forgive, provided a satisfactory outcome is achieved. Sagittarius enjoy a good argument provided it can be resolved. Once a friendship has deteriorated to the point where Sagittarius either does not trust their friend or to the point where they are bored, the friendship will be terminated.

Home Life of Sagittarius

To those typical of the sign of Sagittarius, home can be anywhere they are, whether they are travelling in foreign parts or residing in one place. They may, indeed, have more than one home in more than one country, or several places that they see as home. Those under this sign believe very much that wherever they leave their hats, that is their home. Some influenced by Sagittarius never settle down and spend their whole lives travelling; others travel more in the mind than in body, of course. Home is often seen as a base from where they plan the next journey, and they will rarely be very domesticated or interested in keeping or making a home. Nevertheless, they will have acquired many mementos of their travels and adventures. These will be displayed, and they will generally want an interesting home, with many talking points, which is brightly decorated.

The typical Sagittarius sees money as a potential, as a means for paying for their adventures and travels. As the end is more important than the means, they may well find themselves in serious debt, or at least their friends will find they are good at borrowing. The happy-go-lucky Sagittarius will always find some resources from somewhere as they can be very focused and determined when there is something they want or need. Generous friends and family beware. Most people influenced by this sign will certainly not save for the future; nor plan to pay for a pension: as far as Sagittarius is concerned the future will look after itself.

As mentioned previously, those typical of Sagittarius are very social and love friends and company, and they will want many visitors and guests around to their

house as often as possible. These gatherings will always
be as relaxed and informal as possible, as those typical
of this sign do not like formal dinner parties: they
prefer parties with lots of new and interesting people
for them to explore and discover.

The typical Sagittarius parent will see children as a
new and exciting area to explore. They will usually be
very good and stimulating parents, and will be content
to play with, talk to and instruct their offspring as
much as possible and for as long as it takes. The
Sagittarius parent will enjoy taking their children out,
and will rarely be a boring or insensitive parent.
Generally, they will respect and have faith in their
youngster, and will always treat with them honestly
and truthfully. Those typical of this sign may expect
too much from them, both intellectually and physically,
and they be a bit lax when it comes to discipline. It
may be hard for a Sagittarius parent to believe that
their child just wants to stay at home and doze or
watch television. Being a very active sign, it can be
hard to appreciate another is not.

Children who are typical of Sagittarius are very
active and interested in everything, and will always be
exploring and trying to discover how things, both in
the physical and emotional world, work. This
adventurousness and impulsiveness may lead them into
dangerous situations, and they may suffer from a series
of mishaps or injuries. Sagittarius youngsters are
usually very happy-go-lucky and loving, and are also
very honest and outgoing.

If their parent does not trust them, they can be very hurt and sulky. They will not tend to follow rules when they can see no point to them or where they believe they have been imposed simply to curtail their freedom. Sagittarius children will set their own standards, and the parent should encourage them to do so: a Sagittarius youngster will stick by what they believe. It is necessary for the parent to teach the child that some rules are essential. Youngsters typical of this sign may not, however, express their emotions when sad or down, and they should be encouraged to do so. To the outside, all may be well but the Sagittarius child may be suffering in silence.

They will expect all their questions – and there may be very many on every subject, even ones considered taboo – to be answered truthfully. Sagittarius, of all ages, hate hypocrisy and double-standards, and they are no different in their early years. They should be encouraged to learn and discover, as those curtailed when young may become angry and frustrated as adults. Those under this sign may also be reckless in later years when it comes both to money and relationships.

Children influenced by this sign love company and having lots of friends to interact and play with. They also love animals.

A Sagittarius parent and Sagittarius child in the same household will usually understand each other well, as they comprehend each other's need for freedom and exploration. Two Sagittarius children may be doubly reckless, and should probably be supervised as they may get into all sorts of potentially perilous situations.

Work Life of Sagittarius

Most people typical if Sagittarius are very adaptable and versatile, and they will enjoy jobs where they are allowed to do their work their own way and at their own pace, which will usually be quick. They do not like work which is repetitive and unstimulating unless it can be made into some sort of challenge. Those typical of this sign will rarely get tired except when they are bored, and any occupation which combines both mental and physical challenges will suit them especially well.

Sagittarius is optimistic and usually happy, and they have the ability to boost morale and cheer up a frustrated work force as long as they themselves feel motivated. They may be blunt with colleagues, however, and this plain speaking may irritate some. Those influenced by this sign do not like to get bogged down with details, preferring the bigger picture, but this may mean that they overlook essential areas, particularly if these areas involve dull routine or lots of form filling. They also do not like to commit themselves, and this may mean that they will be evasive when confronted by someone wanting concrete answers, especially for deadlines. They may be rather glib, and simply promise something they cannot achieve to get someone off their back.

Sagittarius is also rarely interested in a long-term career and will want money or benefits now. They rarely expect to be in one job for very long, so the promise of jam tomorrow will hold no interest.

Those typical of Sagittarius are excellent workers where they are given freedom in their work, where their work is not too mundane, and where optimism and openness is a benefit. They do less well where they feel constricted without good reason, where they are to be strictly controlled, or where they are required to make long-term commitments.

Famous People with the Sun Sign Sagittarius

Woody Allen (actor, writer and director),
Jane Austen (writer), Kim Basinger (actor),
Maria Callas (opera singer), Sir Winston Churchill
(politician and Prime Minister of Britain),
Sammy Davis Jr (singer and entertainer),
Walt Disney (cartoonist and businessman),
Sinead O'Connor (singer and Catholic priestess),
Gene Roddenberry (creator of Star Trek),
Frank Sinatra (singer), Mark Twain (writer).

Capricorn

NAME	The Sea Goat (Capricornus)
DATES	22 December-19 January
RULING PLANET	Saturn
ELEMENT	Earth
QUALITY	Cardinal
COLOUR	black, grey, violet, green
GEMSTONE	jet, onyx, black diamond
METAL	lead
ANIMAL	goat, ass

Introduction and Background

Capricorn is the Cardinal Earth sign of the zodiac, and the first sign of the winter, tenth in the zodiac. Those influenced by this sign are concerned with determined, careful and sure, although not always very fast, progress to a desired goal or ambition. Capricorn is concerned with trying to understand other people and the world around them, and they husband their resources and skills. Reputation and status are also very important to those under this sign, along with discipline and paternalism. Capricorn will often believe that they know what is best for family and friends, and will usually give sound advice. They can also, however, be perfectionists and rather cold in nature, and may never be satisfied with the real world and companions or colleagues who can never aspire to their exacting standards. Usually, they have their feet firmly on the ground.

In love and friendship, those typical of Capricorn make good partners and companions, and get on especially well with the other Earth signs Taurus and Virgo, as well as the Water signs Scorpio, Pisces and Cancer: the latter sign is the opposite sign to Capricorn and such matches can be the best or worst of relationships. Capricorn can be bossy, paternalistic and somewhat awkward with the opposite sex, but where there is enough good sense, decency and interest in the partner, those typical of this sign can be excellent and loyal lovers or friends. Where the partner can be disciplined, loving and loyal, those under this sign will be happy with a long-term commitment. Capricorn is looking for an enduring match and will rarely have affairs or one-night stands.

Capricorn is a faint constellation in the southern hemisphere, which lies between Sagittarius and Aquarius. Capricorn is derived from a Roman translation of the Greek 'goat-horned'.

Ruling Planet

The Ruling Planet for the zodiac sign of Capricorn is Saturn. Saturn is a huge planet compared to the Earth, and is the sixth from the Sun. It has a series of concentric rings. Saturn was the Roman god of agriculture and vegetation. His Greek counterpart was Cronus. In astrology, Saturn is associated with responsibilities, perseverance and caution. The serious side of life and learning wisdom through sorrow and loss is also connected to this planet.

Saturn is the alchemical name for lead.

Characteristics of Capricorn

These are obviously general and can be modified by many factors, not least the influence of the Ascendant Sign and the different planets in different houses. Those typical of Capricorn who are frustrated or unhappy can exhibit some of the not so good characteristics, and of course a virtue in one situation, such as being superbly well organised or attention to detail, may not be so good in others. Those who plan meticulously may believe that their way is the only way, while attention to detail can lead to fussiness and striving for unobtainable perfection.

Good Characteristics of Capricorn

- works hard and has many practical skills to bring to any situation
- excellent at planning and organising
- persistent, determined and usually successful, but blended with caution and good sense: Capricorn is sure-footed and careful but almost always gets where they want to go
- capable of weighing and taking risks when necessary
- scrupulous, decent and has high standards
- respects authority, tradition and discipline, and may be somewhat conventional in outlook
- gives good advice and practical wisdom, and is concerned and loyal to family and friends
- paternalistic and caring in a practical way
- interested in fame and recognition for achievements

Not So Good Characteristics of Capricorn

- may believe that their way of doing things is the only way and will become angry with anyone who disagrees
- a bit of a slave driver and scorns those who do not work hard enough or show sufficient dedication
- may be so picky and so perfectionist that they are never satisfied
- unforgiving and critical of those they believe to be lazy, not pulling their weight or with whom they disagree
- tendency to be egotistical and domineering

- may be anxious, fears dominating decisions, and fatalistic in outlook: has a tendency to take all the problems of friends, family and even the world on their shoulders
- keeps ideas to self so that any recognition will come to them and not need to be shared with others: sometimes obsessed with getting fame

Appearance and Health of Capricorn

If someone has personality characteristics which are associated with Capricorn, they may also have the following physical traits:

- small boned but can be well or stockily built as well as quite slim
- when young may actually look older than they are, while when older may look younger
- piercing and deep eyes
- appears never to smile, although has very good white teeth
- narrow forehead, often with deep worry lines
- sure footed and confident in bearing
- very aware of appearance

Those typical of Capricorn are usually healthy folk, although they may have suffered from a series of illnesses when they were young: they become stronger as they become older. Many influenced by this sign take care of themselves and are moderate in most things, and may live to great age. As they are very serious and caring, however, sometimes taking the whole Earth on their shoulders, they can be prone to being gloomy and pessimistic, and may even descend into depression.

Conditions associated with this sign are rheumatism, bone diseases, damage to legs and knees, skin problems, sterility and depression. Those under this sign also often suffer from many chronic conditions, although they bear illness, as with much else in life, with great fortitude. They are, however, often very rigid in outlook and bearing, and this can lead to its own problems such as poor posture and a bad back.

Parts of the body which are associated with Capricorn are the bones, joints and the knees, including the spine, throat and teeth, as well as sometimes the skin. That is not to say that these parts of the body may be especially susceptible to illness or particularly free from it. This strength or weakness can only be determined by doing a full birth chart.

Capricorn needs to learn how to relax and stop worrying about people and the world in general. Many find it impossible, however, to do nothing or to unwind, and they need some leisure activity or hobby, such as reading, to help them rest.

Likes and Dislikes of Capricorn

Likes of Capricorn

- history and old or stately items such as antiques
- books and reading
- privacy and people not prying into their lives

- the best of what there is: expensive gemstones, designer clothes, membership of an exclusive club, up-market cars
- home and family
- duties and responsibilities: taking care of others and advising them about their problems
- being left alone and having plenty of time to achieve things
- sexual love

Dislikes of Capricorn
- being lonely or alone
- untidiness or dirtiness
- anything which comes up unexpectedly, and especially surprises
- being teased or joked about, however gently, and people being overly familiar
- not being taken seriously
- not having enough time to complete things to their standards
- anything which goes against conventional ideas or authority
- feeling that they are not doing a good job or are useless

Love Life and Friendship of Capricorn

Those influenced by the sign of of Capricorn will search for love and a close relationship, and will see this relationship as fundamentally important. Consequently, Capricorn is looking for a close and

binding partnership which they see as lasting for a long
time. Those influenced by this sign rarely want casual
affairs, and they can be extremely shy and awkward
with potential partners. Nevertheless, if they can find
someone with whom they can form a deep and lasting
relationship, they can find true satisfaction and
fulfilment, and in turn can make their loved one
extremely happy and contented. Those under the sign
of Capricorn will be committed and caring to the
object of their affection, although they may seem a
little calculating in who they choose.

As mentioned previously, Capricorn is a sign which
finds it difficult to connect and communicate with the
opposite sex. Many are very shy, retiring and private,
and find it hard to make a move until they are certain
it is the right move: practical considerations are more
important than physical attraction or an ethereal love.
Those influenced by this sign rarely flirt, and when
they do it will be with someone with whom they want
to form a close and long-lasting relationship. Similarly,
they do not feel comfortable making the first move,
and will only do so when they are seriously interested.
Capricorn can be very attractive, however, and many
have a dry sense of humour. Those who want a one-
night stand or brief fling should not consider a typical
Capricorn: they will be looking for a long, meaningful
and committed relationship.

In a relationship, those influenced by this sign are
very private people, and this privacy should be
respected even by someone who is very close. They

may even seem somewhat cold and reserved until someone knows them well, and they are well organised and disciplined – expecting this from their partner. Capricorn may not be very demonstrative, and a needy partner should be aware that when one under this sign shares intimacies, or says 'I love you', although they mean it completely, they do not see the need to repeat it.

Capricorn will do anything in their power to look after those to whom they are close, and will stand by them through thick and thin: not only because they may love their partner, but also because of their strong sense of duty and to do what is right. Those influenced by this sign are also compulsive worriers, especially where the emotions are concerned, and they need their partner to be as committed as they are, perhaps even need to feel that their loved one is dependent on them. Their partner needs to take them seriously and admire them for their talents, and to be both physically and emotionally faithful.

The practical side of a relationship is also very important. Capricorn will need financial, as well as emotional, security, and will usually want to make a safe and comfortable home in which they can raise a family. This may mean, however, they do not choose a suitable partner or may not choose any partner at all, every potential match having some defect. Alternatively, as Capricorn is more concerned with themselves than the motives of others, they may make an extremely poor choice of partner. When they discover they have made a poor choice, they may retreat into themselves, or they may feel quite offended and seek revenge for themselves.

Capricorn, especially when confident, finds sex a very pleasurable and fulfilling experience. They like to please their partners as well, to make the act as fulfilling for both participants. Most see no division between sex and love, and most see no need for sex to release pent-up frustration or emotion. Consequently, those typical of this sign will see no point in casual sex or a casual relationship: they will only find satisfaction in a committed partnership.

Because of their strong sense of duty and doing what is right, those influenced by this sign can find it difficult to terminate a relationship, even when it has become unsatisfactory, and especially where the partner has not actually done anything wrong in particular. They do require their partner to be faithful, and because of this or where a relationship has deteriorated beyond repair, they will then decide forcefully that they should break off. This end of the relationship will be final, and in the end may seem sudden – although Capricorn will have spent a long time deciding what is the correct course of action.

If a partner is unfaithful, Capricorn will approach this practically. If they consider that there is something worth retrieving, they will try a reconciliation; if not, and especially if the partner is repeatedly unfaithful, they will end the match, and may even turn aggressive and nasty. Capricorn has a strong sense of justice, and when this is affronted they may act as judge, jury and executioner: even if they themselves are the only ones to have been sinned against.

In friendship and relationships, those influenced by the sign of Capricorn get on with the other Earth signs Taurus and Virgo. The best matches may actually be made, however, with the Water signs Pisces and Scorpio, and with the Cardinal Water sign Cancer. Where these relationships work, they can be the best of matches; where not, the two signs will just never get together. Both signs have very strong personalities, but Cancer can help Capricorn gain insight into what drives other people, and help them to express their emotions. Generally speaking, typical Capricorn will find relationships with the Fire or Air signs difficult: they are simply not solid enough for the responsible Capricorn.

Capricorn will form long and lasting relationships and friendships with those they see as decent people, although they find it difficult to cope with extroverts. At their most extreme, those influenced by this sign may try to 'father' their friends, or show them deep devotion. While some may like to be organised and to be given advice they are expected to follow, others may find this approach off putting and find such friendships impossible.

Capricorn is extremely loyal and caring, however, and will see a friend through any trouble or illness, no matter how bad it gets. They are not the best judges of character in the zodiac, and may realise some way into a friendship that they have made a mistake. Where they feel they have been taken for a ride, they may be quite judgmental in response and even seek to punish their erstwhile friend.

Home Life of Capricorn

Those who are typical of the sign of Capricorn will create a secure and comfortable home in which they can feel safe and warm. Many will have their home as a bulwark against the rigours of the outside world, somewhere where they can relax and put their responsibilities and concerns aside for a while. Within their home, they will have a quiet corner with all their favourite belongings and mementos. Here, they will feel truly content.

Capricorn is not normally very exuberant or extravagant, and their home will be tasteful, calm and refined, without any ostentation. The furniture, fittings and decoration, however, will always be of good quality and good workmanship: Capricorn does not like shoddy goods. Those under this sign like to be in control, and their homes are no different: they will want to be master in their own place and to control and organise both the home and anyone with whom they share it.

When it comes to money, those typical of Capricorn are very interested in wealth and power. They can be materialistic and will often be concerned with building up a substantial bank balance as they see this a way of also getting power. Consequently, they are very aware of the value of money, and will be prepared to make investments and save wisely. Once they have gathered their fortune and feel secure, Capricorn will be munificent and generous with their friends and family. Some typical by this sign will simply do this from a feeling of good will or paternalism, while others may see it as a way of influencing and controlling people by using their wealth.

The typical Capricorn parent tends to be quite strict with their offspring, and may be a bit rigid and disciplined, although they will always see this as being fair and not picky. Capricorn will try to teach their child to be decent and well mannered, although they will also be gentle, humorous and understanding at the same time. They will do anything for their youngsters, and will try to ensure that they get a good education. Capricorn parents may find it difficult to relate to babies and very young infants, but will find it easier as their child grows up.

A Capricorn parent with a Capricorn child will usually get on well, although problems may arise as they can both be so stubborn. Capricorns of any age do not like to be told what to do.

The typical Capricorn child is mostly placid and even tempered, and in appearance they may seem much older than they actually are. Capricorn youngsters are very strong willed and serious, although they will get their own way by being stubborn or persistent rather than by arguing, fighting or having tantrums.

They do feel more secure when some kind of routine is maintained, and will thrive when their day is ordered, such as going to school, and when they go to bed at the same time every night. Capricorn can become quite serious, and may work steadily and hard at school, using little of their time for play. They should be encouraged to set aside some time to relax and appreciate their leisure and develop their creative and imaginative side. They are often mature and readily accept responsibility and take on others' worries as if they were their own. They need to be shown how to shed their cares, even if it is just to give them a temporary break from the sometimes back-breaking responsibilities.

Capricorn youngsters will not necessarily like large crowds of playmates, and will prefer just one or two close friends. They will also enjoy their own company, and will spend much time happily reading or playing. When playing, those influenced by this sign often like practical hobbies: painting or making things, particularly if they have some use when finished. Nevertheless, they can be a bit bookish and may not have very strong constitutions, and may not want to go outside to play. Indeed, they may appear to suffer from a string of illnesses, although this will diminish as they get older.

The parent of the Capricorn child should encourage them to venture out, whether it is for sport or just to play: to build up their strength for the years to come. Typical Capricorn youngsters may also lack confidence in themselves and may need to be gently encouraged to come out of themselves. Teasing a Capricorn, however, will do more harm than good: they hate not to be taken seriously at any age.

Work Life of Capricorn

Those typical of Capricorn will tend to look for an occupation where they can get authority and respect: often where they can lead. They are usually very hard working, and will be prepared to start early and finish late if it is needed to get the job done.

Capricorns is very reliable, and can manage and will enjoy dealing with complex, long and difficult projects. They are not necessarily the most inventive or are great innovators, but they will rarely complain and will usually get the job done. Capricorn does not like boasting or brashness, and they will try to instil a common-sense and practical approach to their work and business. They will never power dress or wear anything which is revealing: it is not the show of power which interests the Capricorn but the power itself. Those under this sign will wear clothes which are decent and tasteful.

They will always be prepared to take on responsibility, whether managing a project or people. Indeed, this may be their drive in a business: to be in charge and on top.

The typical Capricorn is decent and honest, and this is no different at work. They may stay in the same business for a long time, and will become very loyal to their employer. They will not want to hear a bad word said against their colleagues or their work. They will also expect their work mates to be disciplined and hard working. Those under this sign can have a very ironic sense of humour, and generally will be trusted by their colleagues.

Those influenced by Capricorn will be excellent workers where they can lead, and they will work very hard and for long hours, managing difficult and complex projects. They do less well when being told what to do by others, where innovation and imagination is needed, where their workplace is gaudy, or where a business is involved in less savoury areas or practices.

Famous People with the Sun Sign Capricorn

Joan of Arc (leader and martyr), Mohammed Ali (boxer), Simone de Beauvoir (writer), Marlene Dietrich (actor), Ava Gardner (actor), Howard Hughes (billionaire and eccentric), Martin Luther King (civil rights leader), Mary Tyler Moore (actress and producer), Aristotle Onasis (business man), Elvis Presley (singer), Joseph Stalin (dictator and leader of USSR), J R R Tolkien (writer and academic), Mao Tse-Tung (dictator and leader of China).

Aquarius

NAME	The Water Carrier
DATES	20 January-18 February
RULING PLANETS	Uranus and Saturn
ELEMENT	Air
QUALITIES	Fixed
COLOUR	yellow, violet
GEMSTONE	sapphire, onyx, topaz
METAL	lead
ANIMALS	peacock, eagle

Introduction and Background

Aquarius is the Fixed Air sign of the zodiac, and is the eleventh sign, being the second sign of the winter. Those typical of Aquarius may be unique or unusual in relation to other signs, although these characteristics are often fixed and unchangeable. As an Air sign, however, Aquarius may feel uncertain about

themselves: there seems too little substance in their
being. Consequently, they may feel uncertain about
who they really are, despite being very distinctive when
compared to other signs. Aquarius is non-conformist,
and may have a deep and unique intellect, while some
of their personality quirks may also be eccentric and
even seem bizarre.

In love and friendship, those typical of Aquarius
make good partners and companions, and get on
especially well with the other Air signs Libra and
Gemini, as well as the Fire signs Aries, Sagittarius and
Leo: the latter sign is the opposite sign to Aquarius and
such matches can be the best or worst of relationships.
Aquarius can be aloof, eccentric and opinionated, but
where the partner can be a friend as well as lover, and
where they can respect the Aquarius's foibles, those
typical of this sign can be excellent and loyal lovers or
friends. Where the partner can be open-minded,
honest and loyal, those under this sign will be happy
with a long-term commitment. Aquarius will eventually
commit to an enduring partnership, but they will have
to be certain and this may take some time.

The symbol for Aquarius is two wavy lines
representing water and the water carrier. Aquarius is a
constellation in the southern hemisphere, between
Capricorn and Pisces. The name is from the Latin.

Ruling Planet

The Ruling Planets of Aquarius are Uranus and Saturn.
Uranus is one of the giant planets in the solar

system, seventh from the Sun, and can be visible from Earth with the naked eye. In Greek tradition, Uranus was the ruler of the universe and the father of the Titans and Cyclops with his wife and mother Gaea (earth). Uranus was overthrown by Cronus, his son. In astrology, Uranus is associated with unexpected or rapid change or ideas, as well as originality and intuition.

Saturn is a huge planet compared to the Earth, and is the sixth from the Sun. It has a series of concentric rings. Saturn was the Roman god of agriculture and vegetation. His Greek counterpart was Cronus. In astrology, Saturn is associated with responsibilities, perseverance and caution. The serious side of life and learning wisdom through sorrow and loss is also connected to this planet. Saturn is the alchemical name for lead.

Characteristics of Aquarius

These are obviously general and can be modified by many factors, not least the influence of the Ascendant Sign and the different planets in different Houses. Those typical of Aquarius who are frustrated or unhappy can exhibit some of the not-so-good characteristics, and of course a virtue in one situations, such as independence in thought and action and non-conformity, may be less good in another, leading to eccentricity or even perverseness. Aquarius may have deep doubts about their identity, and although Fixed, as an Air sign they may feel there is no solidity and they have no confidence about their who they are.

Good Characteristics of Aquarius
- kind, loyal, friendly and courteous, both to family and friends
- caring and thoughtful: will often do virtually anything for those who they care about or are in need
- cooperative and dependable
- intensely interested in other people, and will spend hours just watching and listening to others
- can often be very original and independent in thought, ability and outlook
- may have a strong and deep intellect, which can be very original and look at things in a new and unique way
- inventive and often interested in the scientific world as well as the creative arts, especially when ideas or performance are new or challenging
- strong humanitarian beliefs

Not So Good Characteristics of Aquarius
- can be tactless and rude: this is often deliberate and is intended to hurt
- only interested in the self, and may spend much time just thinking about their own lives
- will not commit
- not willing to stand up for beliefs and will often agree with people with whom they strongly disagree
- voyeuristic and perverse in the intensity and depth

of curiosity about others
- can be eccentric and rigid to the point of idiocy
- airy and lacks confidence and may be excruciatingly uncertain about the self
- life can become very stale but will still not take any action or movement

Appearance and Health of Aquarius

If someone has personality characteristics which are associated with Aquarius, they may also have the following physical traits:
- often taller, or appear taller, than average
- have long bones and strongly built
- purposeful in movement
- may have a tendency to have broad hips
- long neck
- have a tendency to have strong or noble facial features, especially in profile
- high and broad forehead
- may appear dreamy and a bit distant or aloof
- when thinking the head may tilt or droop
- female Aquarius tend to avoid female conventions, but always dress to impress

Those typical of Aquarius are usually healthy folk, but they do need lots of fresh air, exercise and rest to remain so. Often they do not get enough of any of these, and may suffer from nervous conditions and phobias. They also do not feel well depending on extremes of weather: either too hot, cold, humid, windy, wet or dry.

Conditions associated with this sign are often to do with the circulation, as well as problems with the blood and nervous illnesses. They have a tendency to get varicose veins, and are also prone to accidents concerning the ankles and lower leg. Aquarius can also get unexplained and sometime severe illnesses, which have a sudden onset, but also clear up equally as quickly.

Parts of the body which are associated with Aquarius are the circulation and ankles, including the lungs, as well as sometimes the lower leg and ankles. That is not to say that these parts of the body may be especially susceptible to illness or particularly free from it. This strength or weakness can only be determined by doing a full birth chart.

Aquarius need lots of rest and to relax in comfortable and peaceful surroundings.

Likes and Dislikes of Aquarius

Likes of Aquarius
- being given the recognition which they feel is deserved
- fame
- spending time thinking and considering the self
- modern art and challenging theatre
- privacy, although they love being set a little apart and even being eccentric
- keeping a diary or journal
- magic, dreams and rainbows

- surprises and change
- credit cards
- ordering other people about, then supervising them so they do what is required and what they are told
- strange and eccentric friends
- being careful with money and not overextending themselves

Dislikes of Aquarius
- being intimate and showing emotion or even affection
- being taken for granted by loved ones, friends or family
- commitments which constrict action
- violence or aggression
- borrowing anything, including money, and also giving loans or lending things
- conventional authority
- people discovering or understanding their motives
- extravagance, either in spending money or way of life
- hard selling: especially ineffective with an Aquarius

Love Life and Friendship of Aquarius

Those influenced by the zodiac sign of Aquarius tend to look for lasting friendship from their partner, as well as love and sex. Those typical of Aquarius may, indeed, be wary of deep emotional involvement. They are determined not to have their freedom curtailed in any way and to retain their independence at all costs.

Aquarius can seem a little eccentric or odd to other people, but they need their partner to be able to accept all these little peculiarities or foibles.

If Aquarius can find someone with whom to have a lasting friendship as well as relationship, they will eventually commit to that person, and will be entirely loyal and faithful. Those typical of this sign will still want a wide circle of friends and interests, and are very individual in their outlook and taste. Aquarius may also be more concerned with the welfare of the group or even the whole of society, rather than the welfare of one significant partner. Someone who wants a committed, exclusive and traditional relationship should probably not consider someone who is typical of Aquarius.

Aquarius usually has a wide circle of friends, acquaintances and potential partners. They will normally approach someone they are interested in as if they were a friend: friendship is all important and it may only be after knowing someone for some time that the Aquarius will want to take it further.

They are very curious and open with new people, and can be very witty and charming. This, however, may hide the fact that those typical of this sign are determined to maintain their freedom, whatever happens. Many are also aloof and seem slightly detached, enhancing an air of mystery and confidence. Aquarius will not want to be friends with or partner to those they find too narrow-minded, or those who say or preach one thing but do another. Those typical of this sign will not consider the standing or wealth of potential partner: only whether they are interesting and true to themselves.

In a relationship, Aquarius will seek to dominate their partner, usually doing so subtly and over a considerable time. This is done so that their freedom is not restricted and they can get to do what they want: they value free thought and especially a wide circle of stimulating companions. This may involve actually living apart so that the Aquarius can keep their own space and stop being constricted. They are also very individual, so much so that they may seem a little strange to others, and keeping their lover at arm's length may also be a way to mask their eccentricities.

In any event, those typical of this sign need their partner to accept them for what they are and not seek to change them or alter their habits. Inevitably, this simply will not work, and will bring the Aquarius and partner into conflict. Once a relationship has been established, the Aquarius will stay in it and endeavour to make sure it continues. Nevertheless, their outside interests will always be pursued.

Those typical of Aquarius do feel the need to unburden their troubles on their partner, but in return they may not be very supportive themselves. Indeed, they do not want a partner who is needy or troubled as they need their freedom from worry to follow wider concerns. If friendship in an open relationship with lots of friends is what appeals, then the Aquarius will make an ideal partner. Those typical of this sign may have little interest in running a home, and may expect their partner to take care of things domestic.

Aquarius usually enjoys and is interested in sex, although they generally do not see the act itself as having much emotional importance. Being a thoughtful sign, Aquarius will take care in relationships, both with contraception and hygiene. Some may be a little modest about their sexual needs, while others see sex as a way of forming friendships – although this latter approach may not be very successful.

Those typical of Aquarius will more often than not be faithful in a relationship as long as they are not curtailed and as long as friendship continues with their partner. If, however, too many emotional demands are placed upon them or if their partner becomes jealous because of attention shown to others, then the Aquarius will break it off. Boredom may be another problem: the Aquarius may breeze off and seek someone more interesting. If this break up does occur, then those influenced by this sign can become cold and uncaring; many, however, will wish to remain friends, even when the physical side to their partnership has ceased. Aquarius will also sometimes manipulate events so that it is the partner who actually ends the relationship.

In friendships and relationships, those typical of Aquarius make good matches with the other Air signs Gemini and Libra, and of course with Aquarius. They can also make good relationships with the Fire signs Aries and Sagittarius, as well as with Leo, the Fixed

Fire sign of the zodiac. These relationships can be difficult: both Leo and Aquarius may be too selfish and self-centred to ever make a connection. Where, however, they co-operate and complement this can be the best of relationships. Leo spends much time enjoying life and doing what they please for themselves; Aquarius sometimes needs to consider the self more, and focus on either themselves or their partner.

Friendships will usually be long and satisfying with Aquarius: provided the friend is willing and able to overlook any oddity the Aquarius may possess. Those typical of this sign like people who can stimulate their intellect, and are not afraid of ideas which are not conventional or traditional. Aquarius does not not normally criticise their friends for their own beliefs or ideas provided the friend follows their own code; they are also open about who to be friends with: religion, status, ethnicity, gender alignment and wealth will make no difference to those influenced by this sign. Friends who do not like to be dominated may also find a long-term friendship has its challenges: the Aquarius may subtly take control and always get their own way. They will put much effort into keeping in touch with those they find interesting.

Aquarius may want to use friends for refining ideas, and may even adopt other people's thoughts as their own as if they had invented them themselves. Those typical of this sign do find people interesting – indeed they may even have a voyeuristic curiosity – as long as the friend does not try to put any emotional demands on the Aquarius. In this case, the Aquarius can be quite abrupt and simply tell the person that their problem can be best dealt with by simply ignoring it.

Home Life of Aquarius

Those typical of the sign of Aquarius view their home as the place where they can be themselves and express themselves fully. This may be where they give voice to their unusual or eccentric ideas. Aquarius's home will reflect their personality. Consequently, if they are quite untidy and disorganised, there house will be the same: they may live in cramped conditions with unwashed clothes and dishes strewn around. If they are sophisticated and ordered, then the home will reflect this: it will be elegantly furnished and decorated.

Either way, their home will be arranged in an unusual way, may be decorated in a unique way, and will be filled with interesting items and mementos. Whatever their personality type, those typical of Aquarius will always like to entertain, and to have a wide range and diversity of individuals and friends around to their house as often as possible. These guests will always be interesting to Aquarius provided they are unusual or quirky – although close friends will always be open minded.

When it comes to money, typical Aquarius is not always very aware of the needs of the here and now, and may not worry about meeting short-term expenses. They can be generous with friends and family, and they may spend much of what they have got on presents and entertaining, or in decorating their home – although generally those under this sign are not very materialistic. This can leave little in the bank for the routine and regular costs of living. However, with their creative and analytical minds, Aquarius will often have savings and investments tucked away for the future or for a rainy day.

The typical Aquarius parent is gentle and calm with their offspring, and will always try to raise a child who can think and act for themselves. They may believe that strict disciplining can only result in harm, and will try to teach a youngster how to think and judge rationally, even if they themselves see the world in a slightly different way than other people. Aquarius is open minded and will always be prepared to discuss even the most difficult and adult of topics with their children. The Aquarius parent will always also want to be a friend to their child, and maintain this relationship right through life.

An Aquarius child and Aquarius parent will usually get on very well, although two Aquarius in any family may act together in a very unusual way, which to outsiders may seem bizarre. They may also get so involved in the world around them that they may neglect their own welfare.

Children who are typical of Aquarius are the kind of youngsters who always have the ability to surprise or even shock adults. Aquarius offspring do not like rules and regulations, and especially being told what to do if they do not agree with, or the see the point of, the order. They will tend to make up their own minds about what is right and wrong, and will usually make sensible decisions even if they have approached it from a different angle. Those typical of this sign are sensitive and analytical, and will want to question everything. In this they should be helped and encouraged: an Aquarius who is shut in will grow up very unhappy and frustrated.

This may mean that they are a bit detached or aloof from day-to-day concerns, or even absent minded. Indeed, on the surface they may seem calm, confident and placid, while underneath all sorts of considering and thinking is going on. Because of all these thought processes, sometimes decisions or conclusions are rather hasty, muddled or based on too little knowledge. The Aquarius child needs to learn how to slow down and consider at leisure before making decisions. For, once their mind is made up, it will be difficult or even impossible then to change.

They may also not be nearly as relaxed and confident as they seem, and parents should give them lots of encouragement and appreciation. Aquarius youngster are also very alert to underlying tensions between people, and if possible arguments or conflict should be conducted outwith their knowledge. The young Aquarius should be brought up in as peaceful surroundings as possible.

Generally Aquarius youngsters do not like people depending on them or breaking into their space, and they may shy away from close or clingy relationships. Indeed, they may not want to show affection or any feelings at all. They will be very gregarious, although will usually want many friends rather than one or two very close relationships. With these friends they will be very generous and genuinely interested in them.

Work Life of Aquarius

The typical Aquarius will usually seek work where they can become part of a team or work with a large group of people or colleagues, especially where these people are unusual. Aquarius, however, may seem quite detached, even where they have got a large number of friends. They will always be well behaved and polite at work.

They will rarely seek any type of work which is mundane and dull, or where they are expected to make executive decisions, particularly quick decisions, unless their analytical skills can be employed. It is not that the Aquarius does not have the ability for management or responsibility, but often they will want to feel free from pressure or stress. They will be very good in producing creative solutions and ideas as long as they are part of a team, and are not expected to take responsibility for implementation.

Honesty is very important to Aquarius as they hate hypocrisy, and if a colleague tries to deceive or mislead, they will not be forgiven or trusted again. It is nevertheless very difficult to shock those typical of this sign, no matter what the revelation. As long as people are true to themselves, they will be respected by the Aquarius, who is the least judgmental of all signs.

Those typical of the sign of Aquarius will work hard, but only as hard as they are expected to or as hard as the job requires. They will also expect to be properly rewarded for any work that they do do, especially if this is over and above the call of duty.

Those typical of Aquarius are excellent workers where they can meet lots of interesting people and will be very good at providing creative ideas and solutions, often having a unique way of approaching a problem. They will be less good where there is no scope for their creativity, where they have to conform to rigid or out-dated ideas, where they are in a solitary occupation without companionship, and where they have too much executive responsibility for outcomes.

Famous People with the Sun Sign Aquarius

Lewis Carroll (author), Ertha Kitt (singer),
Charles Lindbergh (flyer), Wolfgang Amadeus Mozart (composer), Paul Newman (actor),
Vanessa Redgrave (actor), Jules Verne (writer),
Virginia Woolf (novelist and publisher),
Boris Yeltsin (ex-politician and former leader of Russia)

Pisces

NAME	The Fishes
DATES	19 February-20 March
RULING PLANETS	Jupiter and Neptune
ELEMENT	Water
QUALITY	Mutable
COLOUR	blue, violet and light green
GEMSTONE	amethyst, pearl, beryl, aquamarine
METAL	tin
ANIMAL	fish, dolphin

Introduction and Background

Pisces is the Mutable Water sign of the zodiac, and the last and twelfth sign. Mutable means changeable and the sign is associated with change. Water comes in many forms depending on the environment, such as water, ice, steam, rain, hail, mist and clouds. Pisces is also the twelfth and last sign of both the winter and the zodiac: although every ending is a new beginning with the coming of the spring and fiery Aries. The sign is associated with understanding and wisdom for what has gone before, and movement into the world of dreams and the afterlife.

In love and friendship, those typical of Pisces make good partners and companions, and get on especially well with the other Water signs Cancer and Scorpio, as well as the Earth signs Taurus, Capricorn and Virgo: the latter sign is the opposite sign to Pisces and such matches can be the best or worst of relationships. Pisces can be shifting, restless and too willing to please, but where the partner can provide order and a steady stream of affection those typical of this sign can be excellent and loyal lovers or friends. Where the partner is respectful of Pisces, those under this sign will be happy with a long-term commitment. Pisces can be very vulnerable and are not very good at judging a potential partner: there is a danger that they can get used.

The symbol is a pair of fish: two fishes. Pisces is a large but faint constellation on the ecliptical, between Aquarius and Aries. The name is from the Latin for fish.

Ruling Planets

The Ruling Planets of the zodiac sign of Pisces are Jupiter and Neptune.

Jupiter is the largest of the planets in the solar system, and the fifth from the Sun. In Roman mythology, Jupiter was the king and ruler of the

Olympian gods, and his Greek counterpart was Zeus. In astrology Jupiter is associated with wisdom and intelligence, as well as exploration and growth. Beliefs, personal philosophy and education are also connected to this planet.

Neptune is the eighth planet from the sun in the solar system, and is a large planet with eight satellites. Neptune was the Roman god of the sea. His Greek counterpart was Poseidon. In astrology, Neptune is associated with the subconscious and unconscious, and the realm of dreams. Sensitivity, intuition and spirituality are also connected to this planet.

Characteristics of Pisces

These are obviously general and can be modified by many factors, not least the influence of the Ascendant Sign and the different planets in different Houses. Those typical of Pisces who are frustrated or unhappy can exhibit some of the not-so-good characteristics, and a virtue in one situation such as being trusting or mystical, can be detrimental in other: the too trusting can be gullible, the too mystical superstitious. The romantic and creative Pisces may lose touch with reality and escape into a fantasy world of unrealistic dreams. Pisces can rise to the top when they accept the world and turn their dreams into reality, but can also be weighed down by the problems of both themselves and others – and sink to the bottom. Fishes can either sink or swim, especially when battling against the tide.

Good Characteristics of Pisces
- loving and caring with a compassionate and kind nature
- loves beautiful and peaceful places and surroundings
- mystical, spiritual and psychic, and associated with precognition and prophecy
- creative and artistic
- often has a deep interest or talent in the arts, writing, poetry, drama, music and dance
- romantic although can be quite shy
- versatile and changeable
- may be wise and sensitive, and show a deep understanding of others and their problems
- can be amusing and charming with an intuitive and gentle humour

Not So Good Characteristics of Pisces
- can be gullible and believing to the point of stupidity
- temperamental and depressive, shy and timid: avoids stressful situations
- seeks sensation and may escape by abusing alcohol, drugs or overeating, and may seek out dangerous hobbies or jobs
- analytical and looks too deeply into the meaning of everyday life, often without being properly grounded
- too influenced by others' feelings and not strong enough to assert the self

- self-pitying yet at the same time can also blame the self for everything which goes wrong
- may also get too involved in other people's problems
- too much of a dreamer and can lose touch with reality: fantasy seems much more attractive than the real world

Appearance and Health of Pisces

If someone has personality characteristics which are associated with Pisces, they may also have the following physical traits:

- can be somewhat short and a bit dumpy
- give the impression of being clumsy
- the back may be bent as the person moves: they look as if they stoop
- broad shouldered
- soft and caring eyes, which may appear sleepy
- clear soft skin
- large eyebrows
- they may have an odd-shaped head
- short limbs
- may put on weight in later years

Those typical of Pisces are usually healthy people, and normally remain so provided they feel appreciated and loved, and have a focus for their dreams. Those influenced by this sign who are frustrated or unhappy can abuse drink, food or drugs, especially when they are feeling emotionally insecure. Pisces is also vulnerable to depression and other problems, especially when they feel that are doing all in their power to swim against the tide and avoid being sucked under.

Conditions associated with this sign tend to affect the feet and toes, such as bunions, chilblains, corns, boils, as well as deformities. Pisces do not have great reserves during times of sickness and stress, and may have poor memories when about to become ill. They can also suffer from overindulgence of drink and drugs, as mentioned previously.

Parts of the body which are associated with Pisces are the immune system and feet, including the toes, as well as sometimes the lymphatic and glandular systems. That is not to say that these parts of the body may be especially susceptible to illness or particularly free from it. This strength or weakness can only be determined by doing a full birth chart.

Pisces need to relax to be happy, and feel their best when have plenty of time to rest and dream – and of course when they feel loved.

Likes and Dislikes of Pisces

Likes of Pisces

- beautiful places: the sea, beaches, waterfalls, rivers, mountain scenery
- gentle sports and hobbies such as non-competitive water sports
- ambient music and poetry
- being loved and appreciated
- those who require understanding

- powerful or mystical places such as standing stones or churches
- candles and incense
- new books
- privacy and a quiet relaxed place away from the stresses of the world

Dislikes of Pisces
- noisy bustling places or surroundings, such as cities or busy shops
- ugly or dirty places or environment
- being told to become responsible and get a grip on things
- unyielding clothing
- authorities and unnecessary discipline
- those who may know secrets or too much

Love Life and Friendship of Pisces

Those who are influenced by the zodiacal sign of Pisces desire love combined with romance and affection. Those typical of this sign are very deep, although as the Mutable Water sign they shift and move, often restlessly and seemingly without direction. It is essential for a Pisces to feel loved and appreciated; if not they will pine and feel very unhappy and even worthless.

When they do find love, and even if it follows a period of gloominess or even depression, they will be restored and suddenly everything will seem worthwhile. Pisces may seem very vulnerable and fragile, and they do need constant reassurance and to be romanced. And, despite the best efforts of a dedicated partner, those under this sign may still drift off for no apparent reason and find another partner, or may develop and maintain several relationships at the same time.

Those who are courting a Pisces may believe them to be very soft, dreamy and sensitive, and even helpless – and they can bring out the mothering or fathering instinct in many. Those typical of this sign are very romantic, perhaps even more in love with romance than love itself, and perhaps a little too naive and trusting. Pisces, despite their depth, are not always very good judges of character and may end up with someone entirely unsuitable or even damaging, someone who simply uses the Pisces for their own ends. Pisces is very idealistic, and may not even notice when they are being betrayed or abused, simply not seeing the failings in their chosen loved one. They may also put their partner on a pedestal, believing them to have skills and talents they do not possess, then expecting them to show them.

Despite being somewhat ethereal in their wants, Pisces is very adaptable once in a relationship. Once they feel loved and appreciated in a secure partnership, they can blossom and find the strength to deal with all the vagaries and challenges life can throw at them. Pisces usually wants only to please their partner, and are also very open minded. Pisces will never abandon someone because they have problems, or reject them because they are damaged, either physically or mentally.

Those typical of this sign do need constant a stream of overt shows of affection and love to believe that they are still loved. It is very easy to hurt them, either by neglect, disregard or an all-placed word. Any partner should be aware that Pisces expects anniversaries, birthdays and Christmas to be remembered, and to send cards and give gifts. Those influenced by Pisces are very dreamy people, and not usually very practical or realistic. It is necessary for the Pisces that the partner takes these dreams seriously and nurtures them with their own. Pisces are also usually keen to start a family as they cherish children.

Pisces are interested in sex and enjoy the whole experience of lovemaking as it makes them feel close to their loved one. Indeed, they may be more interested in the emotional side of the act, rather than just the physical. Consequently, provided those typical of this sign love their partner and feel loved in return, the physical appearance of their loved one may not be very important. Pisces see sex as an expression of love and caring, although they do derive reassurance from the act. It is possible that they may have affairs or several relationships at the same time as it gives them comfort, and makes them feel needed and wanted. There is a danger that Pisces may be used by those who want sex but have no care for them.

Pisces finds it very difficult to be rejected by someone they care for: this divorce from the person who provides their love and affection is just too painful. Those typical of this sign will want to maintain the relationship, and will change or do virtually anything to try to get it back. They just cannot accept they have been rejected.

This behaviour may be so tenacious and determined that the partner becomes extremely frustrated and despairs they will ever be free. The partner may have adopt quite extreme measures to extricate themselves. It is perhaps in keeping with this sign, that they can simply drift from one relationship to another, without even be aware that they have done so. This may simply be friendships, but may also be sexual relations: Pisces can derive reassurance from a physical relationship, even if it means being unfaithful. This may leave their partner feeling bewildered as they had believed the relationship was going well. The Pisces may well want to remain as friends.

In friendship and relationships, Pisces gets on with the other Water signs Cancer and Scorpio. Good and lasting relationships can also be formed with the Earth signs, as they have solidity and can keep Pisces grounded and nurtured. Those typical of this sign usually get on with Taurus and Capricorn, and they may do especially well with Virgo, although this match may be trouble rather than beneficial. Where it does work, Virgo can show Pisces to see themselves in the here and now, to give substance to their personality. In return the Pisces can lighten the Virgo's obsession for detail and need to serve, seeing that they too need to be cared for. Pisces is very adaptable and can also make good matches with some of the Air and Fire signs, although these may have more problems than is worthwhile: the gentle Pisces may get used. Nevertheless, when complementary, these signs can bring Pisces out of their idealistic world and with energy and drive give the Pisces's dreams some substance.

Pisces will get on with people who make them feel good about themselves and provide reassurance, and friendships can be long and enduring. Those typical of this sign are very loyal friends, and will rarely think badly of someone close, no matter what the friend may do – as long as they do not hurt or neglect the Pisces. Pisces may not be very conventional, in their home, work or love life, and they need their friends to accept this without comment. Those under this sign may let themselves be taken advantage of, although they themselves will not care or even probably notice. Pisces is generally good fun to be with, artistic and witty. They may be difficult to pin down, and their adaptability may mean that they can be confusing, simply agreeing with everyone or not wanting to give an opinion.

As with a partner, Pisces can put their friends on pedestal and almost worship them with their levels of admiration. This huge amount of praise may not be warranted as the friend many not have any very special skills, and may also be embarrassing for everyone except the Pisces.

Home Life of Pisces

Those typical of the sign of Pisces will not be particularly fussy or discerning about where they live as long as they share it with someone or some people who love them and with whom they can relate. This home may be a tiny flat or a huge castle: it does not matter to Pisces as they often live in a fantasy world anyway – sometimes good, but it can also be bad – and their house will become part of it. If they can externalise these dreams, they can create a wonderful place to live. They will want to feel secure enough to let their imagination roam freely, whether in filling the home with fine music, art and decoration, or simply a place to dream. Within their home, they will have a quiet corner or area which they will want to keep as their own, where they can find privacy and peace.

Pisces will rarely have a routine, whether at home or elsewhere, and they may also be very untidy and disorganised. Those influenced by this sign may, however, just suddenly decide that a place needs reorganised and may get to it without warning. Pisces are also very bad at remembering appointments or meetings, and it is usually beneficial to have a clock somewhere prominent where it cannot be missed.

In general, those typical of this sign are not very good with money, as it has no power over them and they are not materialistic. It can flow through their hands like water until there is nothing left – and they are in serious debt – as easily as it can stack up in the bank until it is piled to the ceiling. As in other areas of their lives, they can be a bit gullible in trusting others, especially being duped into making loans or gifts. Pisces may be as equally surprised to find they have no money as to find that they are very rich: wealth just does not interest them.

The typical Pisces parent will probably not be a strict disciplinarian, although they will have rules, which may be regarded by others as somewhat bizarre, which nevertheless they will expect the youngster to respect. Indeed, there is a good chance that the Pisces parent will spoil their child, although they will be very loving and kind. They will always allow the child freedom of thought and will help them develop their imagination. Most Pisces parents will be very sensitive, and will always want what is best for their offspring.

A Pisces parent with a Pisces child will usually get on very well, especially where their imaginations can link and nurture each other. There is a danger, however, that they may end up in a fantasy world, more appealing than reality.

The typical Pisces child is very placid and even-tempered, and they will rarely lose their temper, no matter what the provocation. Indeed, they can be exceptionally good and attractive babies and children. Nevertheless, they will not like routine and will normally be very messy and untidy.

In general, they will also prefer the company of older children and adults rather than their contemporaries. Parents should try to get Pisces to be as organised as possible, and also to understand the

importance of time. In later life those influenced by
this sign may be habitually late or simply forget
meetings or appointments. Because of their vulnerable
and delightful nature, the Pisces youngster may also be
coddled and spoiled – in the long run this may make it
more difficult for them to cope as adults. They need to
learn to reckon who can be trusted and who cannot.

What is certain is that a youngster who is
influenced by Pisces will leave in a dream world as
they have fantastic imaginations which can weave
fantasy and reality into one realm. Pisces youngsters
will often have invisible friends with whom they may
have long and detailed talks and discussions. They will
also see magic, ghosts and the supernatural as part of
the corporeal world. Although young Pisces's
imagination should never be discouraged, it may be
necessary for the parent to help them differentiate
between the real world and their fantasy realm.

Pisces youngsters may appear to be quite shy and
quiet, although this is usually because they are happy
enough in their own imagination, rather than because
of a lack of confidence. There may be a danger than
they will be bullied by bolder children as they will
rarely if ever see the need to fight back. Indeed, they
will never want to lead or even assert themselves,
although other children may want to play with them
and share their dream world. Pisces may need to be
shown that they are important and given a sense of self.
This is especially important as the passive and dreamy
Pisces may be preyed upon by less-pleasant signs.

Work Life of Pisces

Those typical of Pisces will look for a job where they can feel free to express their creativity and imagination. They will rarely want any occupation which is mundane and repetitive: Pisces thrives when they have change and space. Those under this sign will rarely want to be the boss as directing or ordering people to do things simply holds no interest. They are also not interested in in power or wealth. More usually they will be found in a team, where the order and discipline of other people may be a great benefit, or they will prefer to work by themselves. They are usually very good at getting to the bottom of things and people, and can be good judges of character when they turn their minds to it. Often they do not see the obvious because it is their imagination, rather than their intuition, that has obscured the signs.

Those typical of this sign do manage to get work done and complete even difficult projects, although to others it may not be apparent exactly how they have done it. Where a Pisces has no outlet for their creativity or their empathy, however, they will not perform well, no matter what the business. They may simply retreat into themselves, and will appear to their colleagues to be lazy, easily distracted and even morose or depressed. Pisces, being a Mutable sign, can also be effected by the workplace and their colleagues: they may feel unhappy with something as simple as the decor or layout, or take on the mood of those around them.

Pisces will be excellent workers where they have an outlet for their wonderful imagination and creativity, or where they can interact empathetically with colleagues and customers. They do less well where they are blocked from either of these outlets, where they have to lead or take executive action, or where they do not feel comfortable with their colleagues or work place.

Famous People with the Sun Sign Pisces

Johnny Cash (singer), Frederic Chopin (composer),
Billy Crystal (actor and comedian),
Albert Einstein (scientist), Mikihail Gorbachev
(politician and former leader of USSR),
Michelangelo (artist), Liza Minnelli (actor and singer),
Rudolph Nureyev (ballet dancer), Sidney Poitier (actor)
Elizabeth Taylor (actor), Joanne Woodward (actor).

PART THREE
Appendices

In this case, the planets of the solar system are augmented by the Sun and the Moon, making eleven Ruling Planets in total. Some signs – Scorpio, Aquarius and Pisces – are ruled by two planets. The outer planets of the solar system – Neptune and Pluto – were not known to the ancients, and it was also believed that there was another planet between Mercury and the Sun, known as Vulcan. The planets in order from the Sun are Mercury, Venus, Earth, Mars, Jupiter, Saturn, Uranus, Neptune, and Pluto. The Moon, which is of course the satellite of the Earth, is also included in astrology.

It was believed that the Earth was the centre of the solar system, and that the other bodies rotated around it – this is how it appeared to folk on Earth. The planets, however, rotate around the Sun, taking different lengths of time to do so: their orbits are also not round but are elliptical in shape. This means that the Earth is closer to the Sun at some times, further away at others.

Consequently, the planets appear to move through the constellations of the zodiac, as seen from Earth, but will actually be in different positions in their orbits.

These constellations are groupings of stars which appear to be close together, as viewed from Earth, although they are actually millions of miles apart.

This means that when and where someone is born – the date, time and location on the Earth – the planets, including the Sun and Moon, are in a unique (or at least very unusual) alignment. This is the basis for astrology: that this uniqueness can then be used to determine or at least hypothesise about the characteristics and personality of the person.

Most people talk about their Star Sign, although this is actually more correctly their Sun Sign. Although this is an important element in astrology, the positions of the planets in the different Houses, and not least the Ascendant or Rising Sign, can also have at least as great and even greater influence than the Sun Sign.

To predict more accurately someone's astrological influences it is necessary to produce a birth chart, which maps the position of the planets (including the Sun and Moon) on the zodiac wheel at the time of birth. The location on Earth is also needed as the planets will appear to be in different positions at the same time on Earth but observed from different locations. Incidentally, the outer planets moved relatively slowly compared to the Earth and consequently will take some time to move from one House to the next. This will mean that large numbers of people will share the position of planets such as Saturn and Jupiter, and theoretically will then have similar influences in that area of their life.

Sun

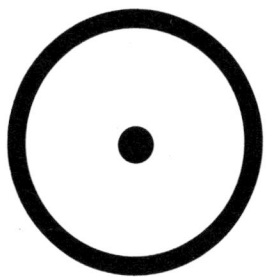

The Ruling Planet of the sign of Leo is the Sun, the star of the solar system in which the Earth is located. Those under its influence expect everything to revolve or orbit around them. Things such as the self, essence, creativity and willpower are also associated with the Sun, along with characteristics such as warmth and pleasure.

Mercury

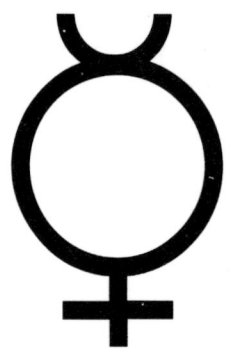

The Ruling Planet of Gemini and Virgo is Mercury, first in the solar system, as well as being the smallest and nearest to the sun. It was known to the Romans, and Mercury was the messenger of Jupiter and the gods (Hermes was his Greek counterpart). The planet is associated with communication, thought, intelligence and mental activities, although those with Virgo as a Sun Sign are more associated with the practical and in communicating such ideas widely. The metal mercury, which is also known as quicksilver, is a heavy silvery liquid at room temperature.

Virgo is also associated with Vulcan, the Roman god of fire and metal-working, whose Greek counterpart was Hephaestus. Vulcan was skilled both with hands and mind. It was once thought that there was a planet Vulcan in an orbit between Mercury and the Sun.

Venus

The Ruling Planet of Taurus and Libra is Venus, second in the solar system, and often visible as a bright morning or evening star, when it can appear blue. It was known to the ancients, and Venus was the Roman god of love (Aphrodite was her Greek counterpart). Harmony, peace, beauty and art are associated with the planet, along with love and sensuality, of course. It is also associated with resources and possessions, and a comfortable home and life. Libra tends to show these characteristics in deeds rather than keep them in their heads. Venus is the alchemical name for copper.

Moon

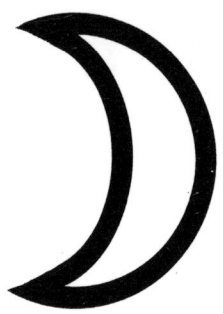

The Ruling Planet of the sign of Cancer is the Moon, the satellite of the Earth. The planet is associated with emotions and instincts, as well as the unconscious and memory. The Moon waxes and wanes, and this is reflected by the changing moods of those associated with the satellite, from elation to depression, then back again. The Moon is also extremely powerful, nothing can stop it from producing the spring and neep tides from the force of its gravity.

Mars

The Ruling Planet of Aries and Scorpio (the latter along with Pluto) is Mars, the Red Planet, and fourth in the solar system. It was known to the ancients, and Mars was the Roman god of war (Ares was his Greek counterpart), who was the father of Romulus and Remus. Those associated with the planet may have much physical energy, and be bold and courageous. It is also associated with action, anger and desires. Mars, however, was hero to the underdog and an inspiration in battles of all kinds. Mars is the alchemical name for iron.

Jupiter

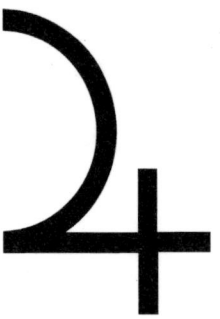

The Ruling Planet for the zodiac sign of Sagittarius is Jupiter. Jupiter is the largest of the planets in the solar system, and the fifth from the Sun. In Roman mythology, Jupiter was the king and ruler of the Olympian gods, and his Greek counterpart was Zeus. In astrology Jupiter is associated with wisdom and intelligence, as well as exploration, abundance and growth. The god was also pictured as being fun-loving and jovial, indulging life to the full. Beliefs, personal philosophy and education are also connected to this planet.

Saturn

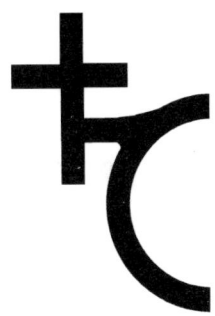

The Ruling Planet for the zodiac signs of Capricorn and Aquarius (the latter along with Pluto) is Saturn. Saturn is a huge planet compared to the Earth, and is the sixth from the Sun. It has a series of concentric rings. Saturn was the Roman god of agriculture and vegetation. His Greek counterpart was Cronus. In astrology, Saturn is associated with responsibilities, perseverance and caution. The serious side of life and learning wisdom through sorrow and loss is also connected to this planet. Saturn is the alchemical name for lead.

Uranus

Aquarius is ruled by Uranus, along with Saturn. Uranus is one of the giant planets in the solar system, seventh from the Sun, and can be visible from Earth with the naked eye. In Greek mythology, Uranus was the ruler of the universe and the father of the Titans and Cyclops with his wife and mother Gaea (Earth). Uranus was overthrown by Cronus, his son. In astrology Uranus is associated with unexpected or rapid change or ideas, as well as originality and intuition.

Neptune

The ruler of Pisces, along with Jupiter is the Neptune.
Neptune is the eighth planet from the sun in the solar
system, and is a large planet with eight satellites.
Neptune was the Roman god of the sea. His Greek
counterpart was Poseidon. In astronomy, Neptune is
associated with the subconscious and unconscious, and
the realm of dreams. Sensitivity, intuition and
spirituality are also connected to this planet.

Pluto

Pluto is the ninth planet in the solar system, and is furthest from the sun. It is associated with Scorpio, which is also ruled by Mars. Pluto was only discovered in 1930, although it had been proposed for some time before that. In astrology, Pluto is associated with death, destruction, rebirth, regeneration and transformation, as well as power. In Greek mythology, Pluto was the god of the underworld. His Roman counterpart was Hades.

Houses are the where of astrology. Each of the twelve Houses corresponds approximately to the twelve signs of the zodiac, and each is concerned with an aspect of life. Each House can be Angular, Succedent or Cadent, and are also divided by Elements: Fire, Earth, Air and Water.

Angular Houses (First, Fourth, Seventh, Tenth) correspond to the Cardinal Signs (Aries, Cancer, Libra, Capricorn), and are the Houses associated with the strongest influence on a person's personality and with executive action.

Succedent Houses (Second, Fifth, Eighth, Eleventh) correspond to the Fixed Signs (Taurus, Leo, Scorpio, Aquarius), and are the Houses associated with stability, resources, possessions and purpose.

Cadent Houses (Third, Sixth, Ninth, Twelfth) correspond to the Mutable Signs (Gemini, Virgo, Sagittarius, Pisces), and are the Houses associated with relationships, travel, subconscious, health and other transitional areas of life.

Houses are divided into four Elements.

Houses divided into **Fire** are Houses concerned with the self and personal life. The First House is associated with the physical body; the Fifth House with the soul; the Ninth House with the mind and spirit.

Houses divided into **Earth** are Houses concerned with the material world. The Second House is to do with belongings and the ability to provide; the Sixth House with profession, occupation and routine work; the Tenth House reputation, acknowledgement and role in life.

Houses divided into **Air** are Houses concerned with relationships with others and the world. The Third House is to do with relationships over which there is no control such as parents, siblings and neighbours; the Seventh House with friends, partners and lovers; the Eleventh House with relationships with the world or with groups such as shared goals.

Houses divided into **Water** are Houses concerned with endings and conclusions. The Fourth House is to do with the end of the physical body; the Eighth House with death and rebirth; and the Twelfth the outcomes and results of the life which has been chosen.

This can be summarised as follows:

First House (Aries) Angular/Fire
Personality, Physical Self

Second House (Taurus) Succedent/Earth
Self-Esteem, Belongings, Ability to Provide

Third House (Gemini) Cadent/Air
Personal Knowledge, Environment, Siblings, Neighbours

Fourth House (Cancer) Angular/Water
Foundation of Life, Family, Home

Fifth House (Leo) Succedent/Fire
Romance, Children, Risk, Creativity, Fun

Sixth House (Virgo) Cadent/Earth
Health, Service, Personal Responsibilities, Work Colleagues

Seventh House (Libra) Angular/Air
Partnerships, Significant Relationships

Eighth House (Scorpio) Succedent/Water
Intimate Relationships, Sex, Death and Rebirth

Ninth House (Sagittarius) Cadent/Fire
Education, Travel, Religion, Philosophy

Tenth House (Capricorn) Angular/Earth
Reputation, Career, Responsibilities

Eleventh House (Aquarius) Succedent/Air
Friends, Groups, Shared Goals

Twelfth House (Pisces) Cadent/Water
Subconscious, the Unknown, Past Influences